PRAYER IN BAPTIST LIFE

Charles W. Deweese

BROADMAN PRESS
Nashville, Tennessee

4269-41
ISBN: 0-8054-6941-9
Dewey Decimal Classification: 286
Subject Heading: BAPTISTS // PRAYER
Library of Congress Catalog Card Number: 85-21301
Printed in the United States of America

Library of Congress Cataloging-in-Publication Data

Deweese, Charles W.
Prayer in Baptist life.

Bibliography: p.
Includes index.
1. Prayer—History. 2. Baptists—History.
I. Title.
BX6337.D49 1986 248.3'2'088261 85-21301
ISBN 0-8054-6941-9 (pbk.)

To

Mary Jane, Dana and Julie,

my wife and daughters

and my companions in daily prayer

Preface

Prayer is basic to the Baptist spirit. In prayer Baptists meet God. And in that meeting, they experience freedom and learn responsibility. They imitate the model of Christ and the examples of other persons of the Bible. Baptists seek to make prayer central to their personal devotion, to their family life, and to their corporate worship. Prayer is the greatest opportunity afforded to Baptists through their beliefs in direct access to God, soul competency, and the priesthood of every Christian. Through prayer Baptists commune with God, worship God, and commit themselves to God.

Baptists often differ in their views of and approaches to various doctrines and practices of their faith. However, they stand on common ground in affirming the values of prayer. In prayer Baptists join hands with the people of God of all ages and places, cutting through religious traditions and distinctions. The ultimate hope for humanity, according to Baptists, is that God relates to anyone who addresses Him in prayer.

The purpose of this book is to present a digest of the Baptist heritage of prayer. Many books by Baptists focus on biblical teachings about prayer, personal reflections on prayer, and guidelines for prayer. These subjects will be addressed in this volume, but the major intended contribution of the writing is to tell the story of prayer as it has unfolded throughout Baptist history. To this point, this has largely remained an untold account. Because this introductory study represents entry into a lot of new territory, extensive documentation has been used to increase its reliability and worth.

The topic of this study is big. Therefore, a high degree of selectivity was necessary. A careful effort has been made to illustrate the major thrusts of the Baptist heritage of prayer by using convincing representative ideas, events, and developments. This illustrative approach is essential in dealing with a subject of this size. The book centers on selected Baptist bodies in England and the United States, although references are made to Baptists in other parts of the world.

Through this research, I have learned that prayer has had more of a shaping impact upon the Baptist past and present than I ever realized. Prayer has resulted in changed lives and has seemingly preceded all the major accomplishments of Baptists. Like Daniel headed for a lions' den, some Baptists have even prayed when they knew that the consequence would be imprisonment and/or whipping. That element of courage and consistency in prayer deserves emulation among today's Baptists. Perhaps this book can help lead to a renewal of the biblical ideal for prayer as reflected in the convictions of Baptists of yesterday.

Laypersons may find this small volume useful as they seek to deepen the quality of their devotional life. Pastors and other church staff members may find in this writing new incentive for giving higher priority to developing a prayer ministry designed to meet the personal, family, and corporate prayer needs of their congregations. Seminary students engaged in spiritual formation and preparation for ministry may profit by using this work as a point of reference for assessing the Baptist heritage of prayer for themselves.

The Historical Commission of the Southern Baptist Convention, which employs me, graciously provided me with an expense-paid study leave in the fall of 1984. This extended time away from regular work offered a unique opportunity to write this book. I spent the study leave at Acadia Divinity College (a Canadian Baptist seminary) in Wolfville, Nova Scotia. This institution (through the special arrangements of Jarold K. Zeman) provided a stimulating setting for writing. Broadman Press, as usual, has been most supportive in this effort. So, to the Historical Commission, SBC, to Acadia Divinity College, and to Broadman Press, I say, "Thank you."

Contents

1

The Meaning and Practice of Prayer

Baptist history and theology make prayer a focal point of the Christian life. Baptist preschoolers, children, youth, and adults have prayed for centuries. Christians of other denominations can say the same, but the prayer pilgrimage of Baptists has taken its own shape. The Baptist story of prayer needs to be told, and perhaps the best place to begin is at the beginning.

The first Baptist congregation arose in Amsterdam in the Netherlands in 1608 or 1609 under the leadership of John Smyth. Two members of that church wrote a letter in 1609 to a relative in London, England. They gave the first (and now the oldest) written description of a Baptist worship service. Centering on interpretation of the Bible, the service included four prayers.[1] These and other prayers in the formative period of Baptist life set the stage for an evolving prayer experience which would help to build a vital denomination of Christians.

Key doctrines of Baptists have made it easy and essential to affirm the values of prayer. The fatherhood of God, the lordship of Christ, the intercession of the Holy Spirit, the authority of the Bible, the sinful nature of man, the priesthood of the believer, and religious liberty, among others, are theological convictions which compel Baptists to pray. Baptists look to Jesus Christ as the primary model for their concepts and practice of prayer.

Prayer in the Bible

Baptists view the Bible as the sole written authority for their faith. How, then, do they relate prayer and the Bible? They begin by acknowledging that prayer is basic to the religion of the Bible. A problem, however, is that "while every intelligent Christian admits the importance of prayer, very few have any accurate idea of the importance which the Scriptures place upon this exercise."[2] Perhaps this book can help make that importance more evident.

The Bible provides convincing information about all aspects of prayer. George W. Truett, famed pastor of the First Baptist Church of Dallas, Texas, from 1897 to 1944, claimed that the Bible is unmistakably clear in its teachings about victorious prayer.[3]

Several noted Southern Baptist scholars of the twentieth century have given special attention to the role of prayer in the New Testament. Thoroughly acquainted with the content of the Gospels, E. Y. Mullins put it plainly, "Now there is nothing clearer in the teachings of Jesus than the reality and efficacy of prayer."[4] W. O. Carver identified Jesus as "the *Supreme Man of Prayer.* Nothing is more characteristic of him. Nothing more arresting. He lived by prayer. He met all his crises in prayer."[5] W. T. Conner observed, "Jesus was in reality a man of prayer. . . . As in all other matters, here the life and teaching of Jesus conform to each other."[6] Fred L. Fisher concluded, "The best book ever written on prayer is the New Testament. The best way to understand prayer is through a study of the New Testament."[7] James Leo Garrett, Jr., asserted, "The four Gospels are replete with evidence that prayer was paramount in the life and ministry of Jesus."[8]

Because of its prominence in the Bible and its values in daily life, prayer saturates the Baptist experience. For Baptists, prayer achieves a special significance at the point of implementing the Great Commission. Matthew's Gospel closes with Jesus challenging His disciples, "Go ye therefore." "Therefore" is a key word. Implying preparation for the disciples' mission and ministry, "therefore" must surely include the training in prayer which Jesus had given His disciples. Matthew shows that Jesus had taught the disciples to pray for their enemies (5:44). He had shown them the proper spirit, nature, purpose, and content of prayer (6:5-13). Jesus had encouraged them to pray expectantly (7:7-11; 21:22). He had invited them to pray for "the Lord of the harvest to send out laborers into his harvest" (9:38) and had set a model example through His own personal prayer life (14:23; 26:26-38,39-46; 27:46).

Is it any wonder then that the famed English Baptist pastor William Carey helped begin the modern mission movement? His sermon at the Baptist associational meeting in Nottingham, May 31, 1792, had as its theme, "Expect great things from God; attempt great things for God."[9] The expectant nature of Carey's prayer life fed his mission energy. And is it at all surprising that a president of the Southern Baptist Foreign Mission Board could claim, "Prayer is the greatest resource we have in world missions"?[10] The Bible provides a basic incentive for Baptists to make prayer support for missions a fundamental part of their faith.

The Meaning of Prayer

Baptist writings offer valuable help in pinpointing major aspects of prayer. Many of these aspects will receive special consideration in what follows. Some questions which need to be addressed are: Why do people pray? What is prayer? What are the purposes of prayer? What forms does prayer take? What are the values of prayer? Baptists have discussed these questions in depth, so let us see if we can extract the essence of some of their responses.

Foundations of Prayer

Prayer presupposes some key ideas about God, people, and religion. First of all, prayer assumes some things about God. God exists. There is only one God. God is personal, present, and active. God is love. He hears and responds redemptively to His people. He is in charge of the world. The roots of these assumptions about God lie deep in the religion of ancient Israel.

Prayer also implies some things about people who pray. To begin with, the impulse to pray is almost universal among people. Human finiteness, weakness, and sin lead to a consciousness of the infinite, powerful, and perfect God. People speak to God because of their awareness that He has spoken to them first, especially through Jesus Christ. Prayer also assumes that people have a capacity for communion with God.

Still another element which underlies prayer is the nature of religion. E. Y. Mullins joined religion and prayer together in defining religion as the most meaningful level of relationship between God and man and then claiming that prayer is the most identifiable mark of religion. In Christianity, religion takes the form of God as Father with Christians as His children, which implies a full and free communication between God and His people.[11]

In relating the nature of religion to Baptist life, Mullins described "the essential elements of the Baptist message to mankind" in his six "Axioms of Religion." The second axiom, which he called the religious axiom, states, "All souls have an equal right to direct access to God." Mullins said that all six of his axioms "grow out of the mother principle for which Baptists have stood through the ages," namely, "the competency of the soul in religion under God."[12] In these assertions, Mullins reflected the theology which had guided the practice of prayer in Baptist life up to his day.

The same theology has undergirded the continuing vitality of prayer in Baptist life since his day.

Definitions, Purposes, and Forms of Prayer

At least three basic meanings of prayer surface in the writings of Baptists: communion with God, worship of God, and commitment to God. The reality and responsiveness of a loving God lie at the heart of all these meanings.

Perhaps the broadest meaning of prayer is that it is communion with God. As "the very breath of faith,"[13] prayer "is the simple, understandable, open, honest speaking of a trusting child to his loving Father."[14] Because prayer is conversation with God, it is central to the Christian pilgrimage of every devoted believer. Prayer is not one person talking to himself. "Distill prayer to its irreducible minimum and what you have is communication; God and man in touch."[15] Disciplined prayer becomes more than an occasional plea for help; it opens up unchartered possibilities for dialogue with the Creator.

Prayer is also an act of worship which joins people to God in meaningful relationship. "Christian prayer is the conscious, urgent outreach of one toward his God and Father . . . with a view to the establishing of a more vital and satisfying relationship."[16] Prayer is a kinship in which there are no distant relatives.

Further, prayer is commitment to God. Writing in separate volumes in 1915, A. T. Robertson, the New Testament scholar, and Harry Emerson Fosdick, the pastor, made this point emphatically. For Robertson, "the very essence of prayer is acquiescence in the will of God, not a demand on God's acquiescence with us."[17] For Fosdick, besides "offering God the opportunity to say to us, give to us, and do through us what He wills," prayer is "a fight for the power to see and the courage to do the will of God."[18] Thus, in prayer faith and obedience come together in the life of a Christian.

The purposes of prayer grow directly out of its meaning. Three objectives of prayer are to seek God, to cultivate fellowship with God, and to discover and act within God's will. Perceptively, W. T. Conner wrote, "What man seeks, or should seek, in prayer is not, first of all, some thing that God may give, but God himself."[19] This attitude nurtures fellowship with God and enables God to work through His people in carrying out His mission of grace. "The purpose of prayer," Conner said further, "is to bring to pass God's will."[20] Or as Ernest A. Payne, the renowned English Baptist historian, put it, "The object of the life of prayer is to keep the gate of the mind open to and to make our own all those suggestions which come from God—suggestions of His Kingdom, His power and his Glory."[21] To pray demands that one be willing to meet God and to respond to His claims.

Several forms of prayer emerge in Baptist writings on prayer. Variously referred to as dimensions, elements, moods, acts, or parts of prayer, no one of these forms comprises the totality of prayer. All the forms have a New Testament basis, and all reflect the mood of the person praying.

Thirteen lists of prayer forms prepared between 1804 and the present were studied to discover the forms of prayer treasured by Baptists. Prayer as thanksgiving was the only form to appear in all the lists. Prayer as adoration, confession, and petition appeared in eleven lists, beginning with the 1804 circular letter of the influential Philadelphia Baptist Association.[22] Intercession appeared as a form in eight writings. Commitment or dedication occurred as a form in four places. E. Glenn Hinson has provided an extraordinarily helpful interpretation of the forms of prayer in his book *The Reaffirmation of Prayer.* He focused on the traditional forms of praise or adoration, thanksgiving, confession, intercession, petition, and dedication. He stated that his book "is based on the assumption that these forms, vital throughout the history of Christianity, still have relevance in our day."[23]

Values of Prayer

Baptists have identified and experienced numerous values in prayer. Sincerity and intensity in prayer have led to these values. In commenting on the meaning of James 5:17-18, A. T. Robertson pointed out that Elijah won a victory through "strenuous prayer and perseverance, not by lightly informing God of his wishes."[24] Spiritual energy has not always characterized the prayer life of Baptists. However, its presence at critical times has resulted in the transformation of individuals; in the rise and growth of churches, associations, conventions, and international bodies; and in significant attention to Christian missions, evangelism, ministry, ethics, preaching, education, and other applications of the faith.

Since one of the purposes of prayer is to enable people to find and do God's will, it naturally follows that a major value of prayer is that it helps make God's will a reality. Prayer can bring about God's will in several ways: by encouraging the person who prays into line with that will, by empowering the person to do God's will, and by helping to make God's will real in the lives of others through intercession.[25] Intercessory prayer can place one who prays so much in touch with God's will that the person is ready for service. A person's awareness that people are praying for him can empower him to do God's will.

Prayer also contributes to the growth of Christian character by making God and spiritual matters more vital to a person. God is no longer a mere theory or doctrine; He becomes a living, personal, communicative Being to one who prays. Prayer can lead a person to acknowledge and confess sin. By bringing the spirit of the Master into our hearts, prayer makes us more like Him.[26] Prayer and sanctification (growing in God's grace) have a distinct relationship. Honest prayer adds to the sanctifying process. J. M. Pendleton, a Pennsylvania Baptist pastor in the nineteenth century, pressed this point: "Those Christians in whom has been most attractively illustrated the doctrine of progressive sanctification have been most given to prayer. Religious biography will support this declaration."[27]

Prayer also contributes to the progress of the total Christian enterprise. A Committee on Progress and Prayer reported to the 1881 Southern Baptist Convention that all real spiritual progress is the direct result of prayer and that every step forward in the Christian life leads to even more earnest prayer.[28] Thus, the report implied that through prayer the Holy Spirit both directs Christian progress and motivates disciples to pray all the more for continuing progress.

The values of prayer are unlimited and defy full understanding. The values emerge in different ways for all who pray with integrity. "Suffice it to say," stated the Shaftsbury Baptist Association in Vermont in 1808 in language beautiful to its time, "by prayer mercies are sanctified, afflictions are alleviated, holy dispositions are invigorated, corrupt passions weakened, and temptations resisted."[29] Or as a more recent writer has summarized, prayer "links the life of men with the purposes of God" and helps "to correct perspective, to restore religious health, and empower for service to men and God."[30] Perhaps the best conclusion is that "a good man's prayer is powerful and effective" (Jas. 5:16, NEB).

The Practice of Prayer

Views of prayer affect personal, family, and public prayer practices. Each of these areas will be explored. Essential to a discussion of these expressions of prayer is an understanding of how Baptists have defined the duty to pray. While Baptists claim that their prayer practices grow directly out of the Bible, they actually interpret the Bible through the spectacles of history. Thus, a look at historic Baptist practices will help reveal why Baptist prayer life has taken the shape that it has.

Duty to Pray

Baptists have long viewed prayer as a duty. Illustrations from several centuries of Baptist life will make this clear. Both the important 1677 Second London Confession of English Baptists and the 1742 Philadelphia Confession of Baptists in America (the first major statement of faith of Baptists in America) stated that prayer "is by God required of all men."[31] P. H. Mell, who served as president of the Southern Baptist Convention for fifteen terms (the longest on record) in the 1860s, 1870s, and 1880s, further highlighted the responsibility to pray. He believed that God required His people to pray to help them check the human tendency to forget God, prize the blessings which God has available for them, understand their personal accountability to God, and pledge to work for the causes for which they stand.[32] The obligation to pray literally saturates Baptist writings from the beginnings to the present.

Baptists have also isolated the consequences of failing to exercise the duty to pray. After asserting that prayer precedes all other duties, a Baptist sermon of the nineteenth century stated that with prayer "all religion originates, and in its neglect all religion expires."[33] C. H. Spurgeon, the brilliant English Baptist preacher, said with concern that "a prayerless church member is a hindrance, he is in the body like a rotting bone, or a decayed tooth, and, ere long, since he does not contribute to the benefit of his brethren, he will become a danger and a sorrow to them."[34] More recently, after affirming that "prayer is imperative for the Christian," James Leo Garrett, Jr., noted Baptist theologian, said, "Prayerlessness is the taproot of the Christian's sins and failures."[35] The evidence of the centuries for Baptists is that Christians ought to pray (following the commands, teachings, and models of the Bible) and that the failure to pray will block spiritual meaning and motivation from their lives.

Personal Prayer

Baptists have long believed that they have a responsibility to pray privately as individuals. Intensely individual prayers of the Bible illustrate the basis for this duty. As early as 1678, an important English Baptist confession of faith called for personal prayer on a daily basis.[36] In 1830 the General Conference of the Freewill Baptist Connection, meeting in Rhode Island, repeated this emphasis in its circular letter: "It is the duty of every Christian to maintain daily and constant intercourse with God."[37] In 1960 the American Baptist Convention adopted a resolution affirming, among other things, that "individual daily prayer" should characterize the life of every Christian.[38]

Since personal prayer is so important, to neglect it can lead to tragic results. Andrew Fuller, key English Baptist leader of the late 1700s and early 1800s, argued against inconsistency between private prayer and the public expression of one's faith: "If we have no freedom in private prayer, but live nearly if not entirely in the neglect of it, and at the same time possess great zeal and fluency in our public exercises, we ought surely to suspect that things are far from being right between God and our souls."[39] Or as C. H. Spurgeon succinctly put it, "We must not be miserly in prayer, neglecting it regularly, and only abounding in it on particular occasions, when ostentation rather than sincerity may influence us."[40] A Baptist church manual of 1859 hammered this theme home even further: "No one can long maintain the life of godliness, in his own soul, or honor his profession of love to Christ, or usefully perform the duties of a Christian, who is not in the daily habit of secret prayer."[41]

Baptist writings identify many cautions against misuses of prayer, private and otherwise. Prayer is not a means of cornering God to do exactly what we want. Prayer should not be used to impress God, others, or self. Arrogance has no place in prayer. As W. O. Carver put it, "Of all places to strut, prayer would seem to be the last."[42] Carver also addressed the issue of "vain repetitions" referred to by Jesus (Matt. 6:7) as something to avoid when praying. Carver first described as a "great danger" allowing prayer to become a "formal . . . set of ideas largely fixed and of phrases that but slightly vary" and then applied this to personal prayer in a prophetic statement which bears repeating:

> If we will check up upon ourselves, we may discover a powerful tendency to fall into the habit of making our daily prayers . . . the repetition of an established set of ascriptions, petitions and reflections. Let not nonliturgical Christians deceive ourselves here as to either our public or our private prayers. We are in danger of being just as formal and just as stereotyped as are those who use a liturgy; and with far less dignity and beauty than the liturgies of the prayer books.[43]

A significant treatment of the personal prayer life is Jack R. Taylor's *Prayer: Life's Limitless Reach.* Taylor urges the reader to keep in mind four points of perspective while reading his book. First, no Christian's spiritual life will rise to stay above his or her prayer life. Second, no church's effectiveness will exceed the quality of its corporate prayer life. Third, no church's corporate prayer life will surpass that of the personal prayer lives of its members. Last, no Christian's prayer life will move beyond his or her personal and daily time of worship of God.[44] In these thoughts, Taylor captures essential thrusts of personal prayer as reflected in the heritage of Baptists.

Family Prayer

Prayer in the family has been vital to the Baptist experience. Baptist associations, for example, have stressed family prayer for centuries. Between 1741 and 1804, at least seventeen pastoral addresses and circular letters of the Philadelphia Association called for careful attention to family prayer and worship.[45] In 1774 the Stonington Association in Connecticut passed a resolution which affirmed, "It is the duty of every church member that has the care of a family to maintain family worship by praying in his family."[46]

The Shaftsbury Association in Vermont often dealt with family prayer in the early 1800s. In 1808 the association concluded, "Right praying begins at home."[47] In 1831 the association lamented the neglect of family prayer and appealed to the Bible: "The word of God affords the most indubitable evidence, not only of its propriety, but of its necessity and usefulness."[48] And then in 1846 this association focused its circular letter to its churches on "Family Prayer." It claimed that "God commands it, duty requires it, gratitude for daily mercies enforces it." Then the association stated, "Family devotion should be regular," "family prayer should be short, simple, varied, and appropriate," and "family worship is among the most efficient means of bringing children to the saving knowledge of the truth."[49] In an indictment that could apply to the present, the association expressed additional concern that "very many, and even some who profess to be the disciples of the Holy Savior, live in the entire neglect of family worship, in order to devote their time to the accumulation of property."[50]

Other associations have dealt with prayer in the family. In response to the query, "Is it not wrong for a man who is a member of a church, and the head of a family, wholly to neglect family worship on account of the smallness of his gifts in prayer," the Kehukee Association in North Carolina responded tersely in 1800, "It is wrong."[51]

Various minutes of the Georgia Association in Georgia between 1798 and 1832 spoke to the issue of prayer. The association urged churches to discipline members who did not hold worship in their families, exhorted Baptists in the association to "let your houses be the houses of prayer," cited numerous biblical precedents for family worship, and claimed that the neglect of "family and closet religion" could rob Baptists of God's blessings on their public meetings.[52]

Individuals have also offered helpful thoughts on family prayer. Robert Hall, an eloquent English Baptist preacher of the early nineteenth century, viewed family prayer as "a natural and necessary acknowledgment of the dependence of families upon God" and believed "a household in which family prayer is devoutly attended to, conjoined with the reading of the Scriptures, is a school of religious instruction."[53]

Irah Chase, a Baptist professor of theology in the early 1800s, presented practical guidelines for family prayer and worship. He proposed a fixed time each day most convenient for the entire family. No "worldly business" should be allowed to intrude upon the devotional time. Prayers should be simple, pertinent, and concise. The conduct of each family member should attest throughout the day to the genuineness of his or her devotions.[54]

Duke K. McCall, a Southern Baptist denominational leader, published some thoughts in 1950 about maintaining family worship. Referring to his own family, he wrote: "That moment when we join hands around the breakfast table to bow in prayer is the high spiritual experience of the day. We simply do not want to miss it. Whatever it takes to maintain family worship will not be too high a price to pay in energy or effort."[55] McCall recognized that maintaining family prayer and Bible reading on a daily basis requires determination, ingenuity, and imagination. To help make this experience effective, McCall suggested that a family select a specific time of day for such worship and not permit anything to interfere with it. Materials used in family worship should be kept in a special place; the family should covenant to join in prayer at the appointed hour even when members are separated from one another; and visitors in the home at the time of family worship should be invited to participate.[56]

Claude L. Howe, Jr., professor of church history at New Orleans Baptist Theological Seminary, reached some important conclusions in a recent study of historical patterns in family worship among Baptists. First, family worship has been a significant part of the Baptist ideal and practice for centuries. Second, regular family worship has not always been easy as evidenced by claims about its neglect in all periods of Baptist life. Third, the focal points of family worship have been Bible reading and prayer.[57]

Public Prayer

Public prayer is "the soul of worship," wrote Franklin M. Segler in the late 1960s.[58] Almost a hundred years earlier, John A. Broadus, whose *A Treatise on the Preparation and Delivery of Sermons* of 1870 continues to remain a classic in homiletics, did not view preaching as the center of public worship. "The prayers," he said, "form the most important part of public worship. He who leads a great congregation in prayer . . . assumes a very heavy responsibility."[59] Similar assertions about the importance of public prayer abound in Baptist literature.

Many Baptist writers have focused on the issue of spontaneity in public prayer versus some degree of preparation and/or the use of written prayers. As far back as the early 1800s, Robert Hall, the noted English Baptist preacher, commented that Baptists "for the most part use and prefer free prayer." He then cautioned, "But God forbid we should ever imagine this the only mode of prayer which is acceptable to God. We cannot doubt that multitudes of devout persons have used forms of devotion with great and eminent advantage."[60]

While Baptist practice often does not reveal much preparation for public prayer, Baptist writers generally agree that such prayer on the part of worship leaders ought to include preparation. Some reasons are that lack of preparation can lead to "indefinite and straggling" prayers,[61] to "stereotyped and monotonous" prayers,[62] and to prayers reflecting "the crude, undigested thoughts of a careless mind."[63] "Not infrequently," according to a valuable book on worship, "one hears some minister in one of these wool-gathering expeditions groping up and down heaven and earth in quest of something significant to say to the Eternal, but finding nothing, at length desists as from sheer exhaustion."[64]

"Just why the minister who spends many hours in the careful preparation of what he is to say to the people should venture to talk to God wholly unprepared it is difficult to rationalize."[65] A pastor with a congregation of four hundred who prays a three-minute pastoral prayer consumes twelve hundred minutes (or twenty hours) of the time of the congregation. Therefore, except for prayer meetings and certain other occasions, praying without preparation "is not, save with the exceptionally gifted, the best way of praying in public worship."[66]

Preparation for public prayer is so important because, as Francis Wayland, Baptist educator of the 1800s, wrote, "it is a more solemn thing to pray than we are commonly aware of."[67] To gain true communion with God, preparation necessarily includes an understanding of the nature and purposes of prayer, a harmonious spirit toward God, and an openness to receiving and living out God's will for us.[68]

Basically three kinds of prayers are used in public worship. Fixed or liturgical prayers are read. Spontaneous or extemporaneous prayers are prayed with no planning. Other prayers are prayed extemporaneously after preparation. The advantage of this last approach, according to Franklin Segler, is that it combines discipline and freedom, planning and spontaneity.[69]

E. Glenn Hinson decried the danger of perpetual spontaneity and called for well-thought-out prayers: "Has the emphasis on spontaneity not led in practice to wooden liturgical prayers recited without thought or feeling . . . ? Do so-called spontaneous prayers not mouth the same trite and meaningless phrases week by week?"[70] After answering yes, Hinson called for "the *deepening* of prayer through self-conscious effort."[71] He claimed that one of the dangers of the spontaneous style of praying is that it can reduce prayer to one form, namely, petition. One way to deal with this problem is to make certain that a service of worship includes many elements of prayer.[72]

While some writings indict Baptists for their failure to prepare to pray; others offer specific and valuable guidelines on how to prepare to pray. One, for example, identified seven ways to prepare to lead in public prayer: to pray privately, to consider the needs to be expressed, to study prayers in the Bible, to study other written prayers, to outline and write out prayers (not necessarily to be read publicly), to memorize parts of prayers, and to depend upon the guidance of the Holy Spirit.[73] Another writer, W. O. Carver, prepared a classic statement on preparation for prayer:

> Jesus leads cautiously into the presence of God. Let there be no impetuous rush at the throne, no thoughtless and irreverent demanding of things, no self-important and self-assuming boldness. A man in need is approaching the God of the universe. There must be preparation for prayer. The

self needs searching preparation and the prayer needs reflection, meditation, ordering. Both in private and public prayer there is far too much of the impulsive, and impromptu, the merely emotional. Jesus bids us pause and prepare as we approach.[74]

Misuses of public prayer include using it to make announcements, informing God of things He already knows, retaliating against or condemning someone, converting prayer into preaching or teaching, placing superficial emphasis on eloquent language, and making too many references to self. "Prayer, like all worship, must be absolutely forthright and honest. It must be relevant to the nature of a holy God. . . . Prayer demands mental, moral, religious, and every other sort of integrity."[75]

Conclusion

The Bible, denominational history, and personal experience are basic sources for discussing the meaning and practice of prayer in Baptist life. Baptists view the Bible as the ultimate written authority for prayer. Denominational history details Baptist understandings of what the Bible means. And personal experience verifies the claims of the Bible and of the Baptist past regarding prayer.

Meanings of prayer include communion with God, worship of God, and commitment to God. Some purposes of prayer are to seek God, to cultivate fellowship with Him, and to discover and activate His will. Forms of prayer are praise, thanksgiving, confession, intercession, petition, and dedication. Values of prayer are unlimited. For example, it helps to make God's will a reality, it contributes to the growth of Christian character, and it aids the progress of the total Christian enterprise. The practice of prayer includes a recognition of the duty and privilege to pray and careful attention to personal, family, and public prayer.

Baptists differ in geography, theology, ethnicity, language, and attitudes. But prayer is one place where Baptists come together in common agreement. Prayer knows no boundaries, and the whole world is a point of departure for conversation with God. Prayer occurs among the poor Baptists of Appalachia, the persecuted Baptists of the Soviet Union, the black and ethnic Baptists of Los Angeles, and among all other Baptists in all other places.

The records and writings of Baptists largely concur that prayer relates to all of life. Prayer has been a conspicuous feature of almost four centuries of Baptist development. Prayer has contributed immeasurably to achievements in stewardship, education, ethics, evangelism, missions, music, and other important areas of Baptist life. While Baptists recognize that to misuse prayer is a grave mistake, they also know that to fail to pray is an even graver mistake. Thus, they continue to communicate with God.

2

The Story of Prayer Meetings

Prayer meetings have been "a characteristic expression of Baptist piety."[1] To determine the exact origin of the prayer meeting as a regular service of worship among Baptists is difficult. Its beginnings in England and America probably lie "in those conditions of opposition, financial and social limitations, lack of trained leadership, and other disadvantages from which all early Dissenters suffered."[2] Meetings for prayer in local churches in the 1600s and 1700s were led primarily by the laity. At first the meetings were sporadic but gradually became widespread, although they often continued to lack a regular time and place for meeting.

A major development occurred in June 1784 when the Northampton Baptist Association in England "issued its historic call for regular meetings, on the first Monday of every month, for concerted prayer for the general revival and spread of religion."[3] Baptists in England and America responded. This prayer call stimulated regularity in prayer meetings, contributed significantly to the rise of the modern mission movement in England under the leadership of William Carey and Andrew Fuller. It possibly influenced the rise of an important prayer call in America in 1794 and undoubtedly added vital impulse to the revivalistic spirit leading to the Second Great Awakening in America. "The practice of a midweek prayer meeting spread in the nineteenth century and came to be associated primarily with prayer for revival and missions."[4]

In more recent years, lay leadership of prayer meetings has diminished. Pastors have tended to dominate the meetings and convert them into abbreviated Sunday services or Bible studies, with decreased attention to prayer. On Wednesday evening, the most usual time for churchwide prayer meetings, meetings of committees and of mission, music, Sunday School, and other organizations have tended to send family members in several directions and to limit full congregational involvement in prayer meetings. A few churches have sought to change two of these patterns by restoring lay leadership and using prayer meetings mainly as a time to pray. Most churches seem to have given little attention to solving the problem of conflicts on Wednesday evening. This is most unfortunate in view of the possibility that children can now grow up in many Baptist churches without ever attending a family-oriented prayer meeting.

For almost their first three hundred years, Baptists commonly set aside special days for prayer and fasting. While continuing alongside regular prayer meetings in later years, these special days actually preceded the rise of such prayer meetings and, in all likelihood, contributed to their growth and spread. Fasting, an integral part of such special days, was a means of self-denial exercised by abstaining from food. While early Baptists would probably have agreed with the recent claim that "there is no evidence [in the New Testament] that fasting is essential to effective prayer,"[5] they likely would have viewed fasting as helpful to prayer on certain occasions and would certainly have affirmed that prayer is essential to effective fasting.

G. Thomas Halbrooks, a church historian, based his definition of prayer meetings on usual Southern Baptist practice. He said prayer meeting is "a relatively informal worship service regularly scheduled by a church during the middle of the week, usually on Wednesday evening, which is at least partially devoted to prayer, and in which the laity usually participate more [though not fully enough] than in the Sunday worship services."[6] We will use this definition. Attention will now be given to the origin, spread, nature, and current status of the prayer meeting in Baptist life.

Setting the Stage

Political and religious oppression shaped the setting for the earliest prayer meetings among Baptists. English Baptist church records of the 1600s present valuable information on various aspects of early Baptist prayer life. The early records of the Broadmead Baptist Church of Bristol, organized in 1640, are especially helpful in describing the formative stages of church-sponsored prayer meetings.

The Broadmead minutes for 1657 state: "We mett in houses, divers times in the week-days, for the Church-meeting, for to exercise the Gifts of the Church by way of conference, or for Prayer in Preparation to the Lord's supper, once a month, or for Prayer on other speciall or Emergent Occasions."[7] No doubt, the pressure to conform to the religious practices of the Church of England forced the early Baptists of this church to meet secretly in their own homes on weekdays for more freedom for prayer, fellowship, and sharing of spiritual gifts.

The church's 1675 records mention a "day of Prayer that we now kept dureing this Persecution every fortnight."[8] Those for 1678 refer to "our Monthly day of prayer, in preparation for the Lord's Supper."[9] In 1680 the church agreed "to change our Monthly day of Prayer" from one day to another.[10] According to the church's 1683 minutes, "We kept a Day of Prayer, as we had for some time Done every other Week."[11]

Thus, the records of this church show that, between 1657 and 1683, it held days of prayer in different years either "monthly," "fortnightly," or "every other week." Some degree of regularity was creeping into the corporate prayer life of Baptists. Other English Baptist churches were also beginning to develop such meetings in the 1600s, although there was some disagreement among them regarding the scriptural basis for church meetings other than those held on Sunday.[12]

A continuing threat of persecution was a realistic aspect of the early prayer meetings of Broadmead and other churches. Broadmead's records show that on January 3, 1680, several of the church's members who had been jailed for practicing free worship "kept a Day of Prayer in Prison."[13] On August 9, 1682, the church "had a Day of Prayer, kept in the open Wood from 9 to 4, where Six pray'd, and 2 preacht . . . in peace."[14] On April 11, 1683, "a Day of Prayer, being a very wet Day, Widow Baldwin gave us leave to meet in her Outhouses, and we were in peace."[15] And on November 14, 1683, "a Day of Prayer, having some hours together in the Wood between London and Sodbury Road, the Enemies came upon us unawares, and seized about 8 persons; but the brethren escap'd to admiration. The Bushes were of great service to us."[16] Thus, the prayer meetings of these early Baptists often took place in threatening circumstances in such uncomfortable settings as prisons, open woods, and outbuildings. Special meetings for prayer were vital to their spiritual pilgrimage, and they did not allow external forces or conditions to hinder their corporate prayer or conditions to hinder their corporate prayer life.

Only a few Baptist churches existed in America in the 1600s. The Pennepack Church was formed in Pennsylvania in 1688 under the leadership of Elias Keach, son of Benjamin Keach, noted London Baptist pastor. The minutes of this church are particularly instructive in showing how a kind of regular weekday meeting emerged in which prayer was a vital part. Shortly after the church was formed, it "appointed meetings for conference to be held on the fifth daye of the week," the purpose of which was "that every brother might have opportunity to exercise what gifts God had been pleased to bestow upon them for the edification of one another." "The usual custom observed was, for one Brother, and then another in order to begin with prayer, and then to deliver their judgment on the text appointed [at the previous meeting], and our pastor concluded."[17] At one point when Keach was away from the church for an extended time, the church "kept up our assemblys both upon the Lords daye, and of conference, spending the time in prayer & exhortation according to our abilitys."[18]

This early pattern of the Pennepack Church was important since this was the first Baptist church in the Middle Colonies and was also a major influence in the founding of other churches. While the church called its regular weekday meetings "conference" meetings, not prayer meetings, the similarities between its meetings and the weekly prayer meetings of many contemporary Baptist churches are remarkable in that both focus on prayer and Bible study. One important difference, however, is that, while Pennepack's conference meetings were intended to build up the gifts of the laity through their leadership in the meetings, in many modern Baptist churches the pastors have assumed almost complete leadership and have converted the laity into spectators.

Prayer meetings of various sorts began to gain ground among English Baptists in the 1700s. Around 1700 the Baptist church at Spalding began to hold meetings for prayer every Wednesday evening.[19] In 1724 the General Assembly of the General Baptists recommended that its churches hold special days of prayer and fasting and "private meetings" of members "that those amongst them who are most likely may have thereby the better opportunity to discover and improve their several capacities."[20] The recruitment of much-needed ministers was clearly a goal of such meetings. Cottage prayer meetings were quite common in the Cloughford Baptist Church during the 1780s and 1790s.[21] Methodists probably influenced the popularity of "experience meetings" in Yorkshire where "from the closing decades of the eighteenth century cottage prayer-meetings became general in country districts."[22]

In America in the 1700s, Baptist meetings for prayer were similar to those of Baptists in England. However, because America's culture was mainly rural, compared to the village and town life of England, Baptists in America had more difficulty holding meetings other than those on Sunday. This may have slowed the rise of regular weekly prayer meetings in this country. Prayer meetings as a normal part of a church's worship experiences gradually evolved from occasional meetings for prayer and fasting designed to deal with specific and urgent needs.[23]

In the Middle Colonies, the Philadelphia Baptist Association, formed in 1707 as the first Baptist association in America, promoted the growth of regular prayer meetings by repeatedly encouraging its churches throughout the 1700s to hold special days, frequently on a monthly or quarterly basis, for prayer and fasting.[24] As early as 1734, the association advised churches needing ministers to set aside monthly days for prayer and fasting "to implore the Lord of the harvest to thrust forth faithful labourers into his harvest."[25]

In the South, the prominent Charleston Baptist Association was formed in 1751 as the second Baptist association in America. It followed the pattern of the Philadelphia Association. From its formation, the Charleston Association recommended days of prayer and fasting for its churches. In 1777, for example, it suggested four such days.[26]

In 1793 the First Baptist Church of Boston apparently became the first New England Baptist church to adopt regular weekly prayer meetings.[27]

Pivotal Calls to Prayer

In 1784 a call to prayer both accelerated the momentum toward regular prayer meetings in Baptist life and eventually helped to move the course of Baptist history toward a higher consciousness of responsibility for missions. In that year, the Northampton Baptist Association in England issued its historic "call for regular meetings, on the first Monday of every month, for concerted prayer for the general revival and spread of religion."[28] Meeting in Nottingham and linking about twenty churches, the association heard sermons on June 2 by John Sutcliff, John Gill, and Andrew Fuller, all noted ministers. Then on June 3, on the motion of Sutcliff, the association approved the prayer call. Although William Carey was not present, historians commonly agree that the prayer call significantly influenced his subsequent involvement, along with that of Andrew Fuller, in founding the modern mission movement among Baptists.

A key factor behind the call for concerted prayer was a book by Jonathan Edwards, the prominent American theologian. Entitled *Humble Attempt to Promote Explicit Agreement and Visible Union of God's People in Extraordinary Prayer,* the book had been printed in Boston in the late 1740s. In April 1784, a copy reached Baptist leaders in the Northampton Association. John Sutcliff read it and became motivated to recommend a call for prayer to the association in its June meeting. In July, Andrew Fuller noted in his diary that he was receiving considerable benefit from reading the volume. Because of the growing demand for an English edition of the work, Sutcliff gave it increased visibility by reprinting it at Northampton in 1789.

The effect of the prayer call of 1784 was enormous. Churches in the Northampton Association immediately began to hold monthly prayer meetings. The association resolved in 1785, 1787, and 1789 to continue the meetings.

The Warwickshire Association made a similar decision in 1786. The Baptist churches in Yorkshire soon followed suit. In 1790 the Western Association joined the movement by agreeing "to recommend to the churches a monthly meeting of prayer . . . and Mr. Jonathan Edwards's Sermons on that Subject, reprinted lately . . . in which such a meeting is strongly enforced, and which has already been adopted . . . by two of our . . . associations."[29]

The pattern for monthly prayer meetings among English Baptists was clearly in place by 1792 when the Baptist Missionary Society was formed as a direct result of them. William Carey, the first missionary of the society, had participated in such monthly meetings and viewed his call to mission work as an effect of the meetings upon his life. He and others even carried the prayer-meeting concept to their mission fields. These monthly prayer meetings deepened the spiritual life of ministers and laity, brought new life to many churches, quickly assumed a missionary character, and continued for many years.

The time has now come to trace the impact of the 1784 prayer call upon Baptists in America. To begin with, John Rippon, the noted English Baptist, printed in his *Baptist Annual Register* an extract of an anonymous letter, dated May 13, 1790, sent from Pedee River, South Carolina, to the Baptists in England: "I lately proposed to our own members a meeting to join with you and the rest of the churches in England, who keep a *Monday evening monthly meeting in prayer to God* for a revival of religion. It was agreed to; accordingly we met, and I trust God was with us."[30] Then in a second letter, dated August 7, 1790, the same person wrote: "I have now to inform you, that *several churches* have been prevailed on to adopt the monthly meeting of prayer."[31] These letters clearly show that the monthly prayer meetings resulting from the prayer call of 1784 were beginning to take place in America.

In its September 1794 meeting, the Kehukee Baptist Association in North Carolina "resolved that the Saturday before the fourth Sunday in every month should be appointed a day for *prayer meetings* throughout the churches . . . to make earnest prayer to God for a revival of religion amongst us."[32] While the day of the week suggested for prayer meetings was Saturday instead of the Monday followed in the pattern of Baptists in England and South Carolina, the call for such meetings on a monthly basis was the same, as was the intended purpose of the meetings.

In 1794 twenty-three New England ministers issued an extremely influential call to prayer in the form of a circular letter. Among the sponsoring ministers were Stephen Gano and Isaac Backus, both prominent Baptist leaders. It is difficult to document the precise factors leading to the formulation of this call for ministers and churches to pray for revival. However, the growing impact of the Northampton prayer call of only ten years earlier may possibly have been at least one factor. Addressed to "the ministers and churches of every Christian denomination in the United States" and intended to unite them "in extraordinary prayer for the revival of religion and the advancement of Christ's Kingdom on earth," the circular letter urged them to conduct prayer meetings "on every first Tuesday, of the four quarters of the year, beginning with the first Tuesday of January, 1795, at two o'clock in the afternoon."[33] They were also encouraged to continue such a "plan of concert . . . from quarter to quarter, and from year to year, until . . . we shall obtain the blessing for which we pray."[34]

One researcher has cited evidence to show that certain Dutch Reformed, Methodist, Moravian, and Presbyterian leaders and churches soon began to implement this prayer call.[35] Baptists were also sensitive to it and quickly began to put it into practice in New England, the Middle States, and the South.

In 1795 at least three Baptist associations in New England

recommended that their churches heed the prayer call of 1794 by joining in a quarterly concert of prayer. These were the Warren Association of Rhode Island,[36] the Leyden Association of Vermont,[37] and the Shaftsbury Association of Vermont.[38] A historian of the Shaftsbury Association wrote in 1853 that this action by the association "was but a few years after our brethren in England . . . had begun what has been called the 'Monthly Concert' of prayer for the spread of the Gospel in the world; and we presume it was suggestive of this quarterly concert during this associational year."[39] The association's circular letter of 1808 had also acknowledged an awareness of the influence of the English Baptist prayer call of 1784 when it stated that the Northampton Baptist Association had "established a prayer meeting, for the spread of the gospel and for the success of missions. It has been greatly blessed."[40]

The Philadelphia Association was the most influential association in the Middle States. Prior to the prayer call of 1794, it had recommended quarterly days of prayer and fasting to its churches in at least the following years: 1756-1762, 1773-1776, and 1778-1780.[41] The recommendations usually called for the days to be held on Thursday or Friday to pray for such concerns as war with England, personal sin, and the need for general revival.

Affected by the prayer call of 1794, the association changed its recommendation in 1795 as follows: "In conformity to the general concert for prayer, in which many churches have engaged,—We appoint and recommend the first Tuesday in January, April, July, and October, beginning at two o'clock, P.M., particularly to implore a blessing on the Word, and the general spread of the Gospel."[42] The association made similar recommendations to its churches in 1797 and in each year from 1800 to 1807.[43] The net result of these recommendations was that the association established a strong base for quarterly prayer meetings in its churches.

In the South, two Baptist associations which recommended the 1794 quarterly prayer call to their churches in the 1790s were the Georgia Association in Georgia[44] and the Charleston Association in South Carolina.[45] In the First Baptist Church of Charleston, which had introduced the quarterly prayer meetings to the Charleston Association, the practice "fell into disuse about 1810." "The church soon after set up the *Monthly Concert* of prayer, on the first Monday evening in every month, which had been first established by our brethren in England of the Nottingham Association [Northampton Association in Nottingham], June 3, 1784."[46]

After 1800 there seemed to be a return, in places other than Charleston, to more frequent monthly prayer meetings, after the English Baptist pattern initiated in 1784 and soon transplanted to America. For example, the Sandy Creek Baptist Association in North Carolina recommended to its churches in 1816 that they observe "the monthly concert of prayer, on the evening of the first Monday in every month, for the spread of the gospel."[47] The Triennial Convention, the first national body of Baptists in America, voted in 1817 to recommend to its churches that they observe the first Monday in every month as a day of prayer for missions.[48] The Cahawba Baptist Association in Alabama recommended a monthly concert of prayer to its churches in 1826 in which it made direct reference to the English Baptist heritage for prayer meetings. This recommendation is significant because it reveals the long-term influence upon Baptists in America of the Northampton prayer call forty-two years earlier. The recommendation described the intended purposes of such meetings in the early 1800s and suggested an alternative to churchwide prayer meetings. Therefore, a major portion of the recommendation follows:

> By a memorial from the Big Creek church it is earnestly recommended to the churches of our union, for the members

> to observe the Monthly Concert for social prayer, on the first Monday evening in every month. This concert was commenced by the English Baptists about 31 [actually 42] years ago, and has been continued by our worthy brethren in England and America to the present time. The objects of these meetings are—to unite in prayer for a revival of religion in our churches, for an increase of gospel ministers, for the spread of the gospel among the heathens, and for the salvation of poor sinners to the end of the earth. Where it is not convenient for whole churches to assemble at their places of worship, it is recommended to hold society meetings in different neighborhoods.[49]

More Recent Developments

New prayer-meeting patterns began to emerge among Baptists in the United States as the 1800s unfolded. First, monthly and quarterly prayer meetings for missions declined in the latter half of the century. Second, weekly prayer meetings for entire congregations gained strength and became quite common. Third, special-emphasis prayer meetings began to be held by such groups as women, young people, and Sunday School supporters. Fourth, churches began to turn the leadership of prayer meetings over to pastors and to lessen the leadership of laypersons in the meetings.

Scattered efforts continued to be made to promote monthly and quarterly concerts of prayer for missions. For example, both the Hudson River Baptist Association in New York in 1829 and the Louisiana Baptist State Convention in 1860 recommended monthly prayer meetings to their churches.[50] However, the general trend was toward a decline of such meetings. The decline seemed to take hold during the era of Civil War and Reconstruction. When Edward T. Hiscox released his *The Baptist Church Directory* in 1859, he noted that monthly prayer meetings for missions were being used "quite extensively by the churches."[51] When Hiscox's *The New Directory for Baptist Churches* was released only thirty-five years later, it stated that the monthly concert of prayer for missions "seems falling into neglect."[52]

In the Southern Baptist Convention, monthly prayer meetings for missions clearly lost much of their prominence by the 1880s. The 1881 adopted report of the Convention's Committee on Progress and Prayer attributed a widespread decay of interest in missions primarily to "the abandonment of the monthly concert of prayer" and then urged "the re-establishment of the Monthly Concert of Prayer in each church throughout the bounds of our Convention."[53]

Later the 1883 adopted report of the Convention's committee which studied the conclusions of the Foreign Mission Board's report called for "more special services of prayer for missions," admitting, however, that it "may not be practicable to re-establish the old monthly concert of prayer." In its place the committee called for each church to hold *"a monthly missionary meeting"* at which information about missions could be shared and special prayer for missions could be made.[54] The 1888 Convention adopted a committee report which stated, "We earnestly urge the establishment and maintenance of the monthly concert of prayer for missions."[55] The 1892 report of the Convention's Foreign Mission Board reported an increase of interest in world missions and cited as one reason that "many pastors have revived the monthly concert of prayer."[56] This development was temporary, however, for new approaches to prayer and missions were beginning to take hold in Southern Baptist life.

A second major pattern in the 1800s focused on the expansion of regular weekly prayer meetings in churches. To determine the exact starting point for such meetings in Baptist life is virtually impossible. Occasional evidence of various kinds of weekly prayer meetings, usually held on a sporadic basis, shows their existence in the 1700s. The Pennepack Church in Pennsylvania had its weekly "conference" meetings, which included prayer, as early as the 1680s. Perhaps the first Baptist church, at least in New England, to have regular weekly prayer meetings according to the approach familiar to Baptists today was the First Baptist Church of Boston; it adopted the practice on October 28, 1793. The church first held the meetings on Monday evenings but soon changed to Wednesday evenings.[57]

The following can help show how weekly prayer meetings spread geographically and chronologically across the United States during the 1800s. Weekly prayer meetings existed in the First Baptist Church of Richmond, Virginia, by 1811; in the First Baptist Church of Nashville, Tennessee, by 1831; and in some churches in Oregon by the 1850s.[58] As early as 1824, the Georgia Baptist Convention minutes recorded that "weekly and concert prayer meetings are constantly kept up and promptly attended."[59] And in 1829 the General Conference of the Freewill Baptists called upon its churches "to consider it their indispensable duty, where conveniently situated, to hold, and faithfully attend, weekly prayer, or conference meetings."[60] Thus, by the 1820s regular weekly prayer meetings were becoming an important part of Baptist church life in this country.

A third pattern was the growth of specialized prayer meetings by various groups within churches. For example, women's prayer meetings for missionary purposes became extremely popular. In behalf of the Boston Female Society for Missionary Purposes, secretary Mary Webb prepared an address dated February 3, 1812, for distribution to women in several denominations. The address entered Baptist life through publication in *The Massachusetts Baptist Missionary Magazine* in March 1812. The significance of the address was that it called for women's societies across the country "to set apart the first Monday afternoon of every month, for solemn prayer to God, for the out-pouring of his Holy Spirit, a general revival of pure and undefiled religion, and a universal spread of the gospel."[61]

In another address one year later, Mary Webb wrote that the Boston Female Society had received letters from a number of female societies of several denominations "expressing their warmest approbation of our proposals, and their determination to unite in concert with us."[62] One evidence of the impact of the appeal upon Baptist life was that certain women in the First Baptist Church of Richmond, Virginia, responded favorably to it in 1813 by forming a woman's missionary society, the first such society among Baptist women in Virginia.[63]

Women's prayer meetings continued throughout the 1800s. In 1851 women in the First Baptist Church of Philadelphia held such a meeting every Tuesday afternoon.[64] In 1859 Hiscox reported that women in "many churches" were holding weekly meetings for prayer.[65] Hiscox's church manual of 1894 indicated that these meetings were continuing and identified an important reason why women were holding their own prayer meetings. Basically, they felt "more freedom than in the general meetings" because their own prayer meetings provided "occasion for those to exercise their gifts who lack the courage, or possibly doubt the propriety of females speaking in . . . assemblies."[66]

Young people's prayer meetings also grew. To illustrate, Hiscox wrote in 1859 that young people in many churches were holding such weekly meetings.[67] The Roanoke Baptist Association in Virginia recorded in its 1859 minutes that a young men's prayer meeting had arisen in one of its churches.[68] By 1874 a young people's prayer meeting existed in the First Baptist Church of Montgomery, Alabama.[69] The Hiscox church manual of 1894 said, "The young people's prayer-meeting is now almost everywhere in the churches."[70] Prayer meetings for youth perhaps grew in reaction to the predominantly adult orientation of many regular church prayer meetings.

Sunday School prayer meetings, held on various days of the week, also emerged. They were fairly widespread by the end of the 1800s. Hiscox stated in 1894, "Sunday-school work has become so wide-spread, so vital as a religious agency, and so efficient among the young, that it rightly holds a large place in the sympathies and prayers of the churches."[71]

A fourth pattern among Baptists in the 1800s was to turn over the leadership of churchwide prayer meetings to pastors and to lessen the leadership role of laypersons. An 1879 manual on the qualifications and duties of Baptist ministers asserted that the pastor should ordinarily conduct prayer meetings because "no other can so fully understand the condition of those present, or so wisely adapt the exercise to their needs." The manual further claimed that because continuity in "instruction and spirit" should exist between the Sunday sermon and the weekly prayer meeting, "one mind . . . should direct and inspire both."[72] The Hiscox manual of 1894 virtually agreed with these conclusions in its statement that the pastor "ought not to commit the management of so important a matter to other hands, as a rule."[73]

The position reflected in these manuals represented a departure from the spirit of early Baptist life when prayer meetings provided a setting in which laypersons could exercise their spiritual gifts and churches could cultivate potential ministers. As pastors began to convert weekly prayer meetings into mini-Sunday worship services, laypeople began to lose an opportunity to enhance their own leadership skills. While one could argue that the proliferation of various special-purpose prayer meetings may have worked against the strength of churchwide prayer meetings, one could develop an equally compelling case that the gradual diminishing of the leadership role of laypersons in churchwide prayer meetings may have stimulated them to form other kinds of prayer meetings which could more effectively meet their needs.

Many of the prayer-meeting patterns established in the late 1800s became so entrenched in Baptist life that they continue to the present. Weekly churchwide prayer meetings are common and are usually led by pastors. Special-interest prayer meetings by groups within churches still exist. Typically only a small percentage of church members attend weekly prayer meetings. Midweek prayer meetings face the additional problem of competing meetings of other kinds during the same hour. Some churches, however, are making earnest efforts to reinvigorate their prayer meetings with creative approaches, including renewed attention to lay leadership.

Conclusion

Baptist prayer meetings arose in the 1600s, often in the context of religious and political suppression. Whether in private homes, in forests, or even in prisons, Baptists boldly countered the bondage of persecution by expressing themselves freely in prayer. Frequently devoid of ministerial leadership, untrained laypersons conducted their own prayer meetings. At first, they lacked regular times and places for such meetings, but they used their times together to great advantage. In special settings of prayer, church members prepared for celebrations of the Lord's Supper, exercised their spiritual gifts, sought out and cultivated potential ministers, expounded on biblical texts, and spent considerable amounts of time praying. Regularly scheduled meetings for prayer became more prevalent in the late 1700s and early 1800s.

The 1784 prayer call of the Northampton Baptist Association in England significantly altered the nature of Baptist prayer meetings by adding a strong missionary character to them. Emphasizing regular monthly meetings and having wide influence among Baptists in several parts of the world, this prayer call appeared at a teachable moment in the story of Baptists. It contributed to the rise of a national missionary organization among the Baptists in England in 1792; it possibly influenced the rise of a similar prayer call among Baptists in the United States in 1794. The English prayer call was a factor behind the Second Great Awakening at the turn of the 1800s. It was adopted by the first national body of Baptists in the United States in 1817; it became perhaps the most important incentive for the international emergence of regularly scheduled, missions-oriented prayer meetings in Baptist church life.

As the 1800s progressed, new patterns in prayer began to appear. Monthly and quarterly prayer meetings for missions and other causes began to decline toward the end of the century. Weekly prayer meetings became more common. Special prayer meetings by women, youth, Sunday School supporters, and other groups gained momentum. The role of lay leaders in prayer meetings began to lessen as the role of ordained ministers became more prominent.

What about the twentieth century? Weekly prayer meetings became the order of the day in much Baptist life. In recent years, the multiplication of other midweek meetings in churches has weakened the status of prayer meetings in many churches. Some churches are making creative attempts to ensure that the meetings are meaningful worship events. While prayer meetings in many churches lack the vitality and priority that such meetings once had among Baptists, hundreds of thousands of Baptists continue to enjoy weekly communion with God in such meetings.

Reflecting on the history of prayer in Baptist life, Ernest A. Payne stated, "The verdict of history is clear, [prayer meetings have been] a characteristic expression of Baptist piety and they have created as well as registered spiritual conviction and power."[74] So, although Baptists have approached prayer meetings in different ways and with varying emphases, they have generally viewed them as grounded in Scripture and as rooted in the Baptist spirit.

3

Special Prayer Emphases

In addition to hammering out their views of prayer and working out their approaches to regular prayer meetings, Baptists have sponsored special prayer emphases throughout their history. These emphases have found expression in such developments as moments of prayer, hours of prayer, days of prayer, weeks of prayer, and seasons of prayer. Concerts of prayer, prayer vigils, calls to prayer, cycles of prayer, chains of prayer, and prayer crusades have also been encouraged. Individuals and groups have used prayer diaries, prayer calendars, prayer cards, prayergrams, prayer lists, prayer letters, and prayer alerts. Churches and others have established prayer rooms, prayer closets, intercessory prayer lines, intercessory prayer leagues, prayer plans, prayer gardens, prayer retreats, prayer support teams, prayer partners, prayer mates, prayer groups, and prayer ministries. Recent developments include prayer fellowships, prayer breakfasts, prayer brunches, prayer luncheons, prayer banquets, prayer covenants, prayer conferences, prayer seminars, prayer committees, and even endowed chairs of prayer.

These emphases represent the efforts of Baptists to relate prayer creatively to many phases of life. Therefore, in this chapter, we will explore the application of several of these special emphases in different areas of Baptist life. We will look at ways Baptists have cultivated prayer in the areas of missions, evangelism, and revivalism; cooperative relationships, peace, and other ethical concerns; and national meetings of Baptist conventions, colleges, and seminaries. Other special emphases that will be highlighted are stewardship, the family, and local church prayer ministries. Examination of these topics will clearly show that prayer always has been and continues to be foundational in Baptist life.

Before opening up these areas, however, we need to explore in some detail a feature of prayer life which, while vital to Baptists in their first three hundred years, has almost become a forgotten discipline in the twentieth century. That discipline is fasting. The primary way that Baptists engaged this discipline was to appoint special days for prayer and fasting. The fact that fasting had a vital connection to the prayer story of Baptists in the first three quarters of their history is ample reason to lay out this story and then ask, Where did fasting go? Why?

Prayer and Fasting

From their earliest days until the early 1900s, Baptists regularly fasted on days of prayer for special occasions. Beginning with the General Baptist confession of 1611, several major English Baptist confessions of faith of the 1600s recommended fasting, along with prayer and the laying on of hands, as an essential part of the ordination of certain church officers.[1] Patterned after the Second London Confession of 1677, the Philadelphia Confession was adopted in 1742 by the Philadelphia Baptist Association. It was the first major confession of Baptists in America and suggested prayer, fasting, and the laying on of hands for the ordination of bishops or elders.[2] The Philadelphia Confession was highly influential in America into the 1800s. Neither the important New Hampshire Baptist Confession of 1833 nor the statements of faith adopted by the Southern Baptist Convention in 1925 and 1963 mentioned fasting.

Several writings prepared by Baptists in England and

America between 1678 and 1818 describe the nature and purpose of fasting. Thomas Grantham, an English Baptist of the 1600s, asserted a biblical basis for fasting and called it a Christian duty. According to him, a pastor or other leading men in a church, with the consent of the congregation, could call a fast, which involved abstinence from food for one day. The purposes were to control sin, reform lives, and relax the judgments of God.[3]

Adam Taylor, historian of the English General Baptists, described fasting among these Baptists during the 1600s as meaning complete abstinence from food, pleasure, and work for one day, usually from 6:00 AM to 6:00 PM. Baptists used this time to read the Bible, pray, preach, and perform acts of charity and mercy. Fasting was used especially in electing and ordaining church officers, although it was often used on other occasions.[4]

Morgan Edwards, first historian of Baptists in America, wrote in 1774 that occasions for fasting other than the ordination of church officers included times of threatening danger, of public evil, and of soliciting blessings from God. Prayer, humility, and affliction of soul were vital to fasting.[5]

In 1779 Abel Morgan, pastor of the Middletown Baptist Church in New Jersey, identified Matthew 6:16 as a New Testament basis for fasting. He then divided religious fasts into two types: private (when one person could choose to fast and pray alone) and public (which could be appointed by a civil power or by mutual agreement of the members of a church). Fasting was to be accompanied by confession of sin, prayer, humiliation, and acts of kindness to the needy. Occasions for fasting and prayer were to avert the judgments of God expressed through "sword, famine, pestilence, or other sore afflictions"; to entreat revival, success for the gospel, and other blessings; and to undertake such important events as constituting churches, ordaining church officers, and preparing for the Lord's Supper.[6]

When a civil ruler appointed a public fast, churches of all denominations were expected to comply by stopping all travel, recreation, and work. They were also to observe such a day as a legal holy day like Sunday, including holding a worship service where the proclamation to fast would be read. Isaac Backus, for example, noted Massachusetts Baptist pastor in the late 1700s, normally cooperated in such fasts, despite his strong belief in the separation of church and state.[7] Backus also practiced private fasting as evidenced by entries in his diary both before and after he became a Baptist.[8]

In an 1811 sermon, a South Carolina Baptist pastor helpfully revealed the nature and design of fasting. After stating that "abstinence from meat and drink does not constitute the principal part of a fast," he said that a fast is "a day of solemn and extraordinary prayer;—of extraordinary devotion;—confession and humiliation." To be sure, he continued, "Fasting, unconnected with prayer, will be of no avail in the sight of God."[9] The purposes of fasting were to alleviate divine displeasure, to avert the judgments of God, to plead with God for persons in distress, to seek God's direction in difficult times, to secure divine help in dealing with important matters, and to humble the body into subjection to the soul.[10]

A common practice among early Baptist churches, associations, and larger bodies was to set aside special days for prayer and fasting. Early English Baptist churches frequently established days for prayer and fasting and thus laid the foundation for this practice in Baptist life. Four churches in the 1600s and early 1700s at Fenstanton, Bristol, Amersham, and Ford or Cuddington were among these. In the 1650s, the Fenstanton Church set apart several such days to choose and ordain church officers.[11] In 1658 the church disciplined one member because he was "absent from the congregation on the fast day . . . being at a foolish foot-ball play."[12] In that same year, the church held another fast day "to seek the Lord" on behalf of "Mary Coxe [who] was greatly afflicted with heavy temptations."[13]

Between 1662 and 1679, the Broadmead Church in Bristol appointed days of prayer, which often included fasting, to set apart pastors, ruling elders, deacons, and deaconesses, to prepare for the Lord's Supper, to pray for a member who was seriously ill, to discipline errant members, to pray for a member addicted to alcoholic beverage, to hear preaching, to confess sins, and to approve persons to be admitted into church membership.[14]

The Amersham Church held numerous days of prayer and fasting between 1675 and 1682. The time of day was usually 6:00 AM to 6:00 PM. Some of the purposes were to renew spiritual commitments, to cultivate a spirit of love, to pray for a good harvest, to beseech God's protection from civil and religious authorities, to seek God's mercies, to confess personal and national sins, to request God to hasten the coming of His kingdom, to pray for courage if called to suffer, and to ask God to bring forth more ministers.[15]

From 1703 to 1718, the church at Ford or Cuddington held days of prayer and fasting to restore to full membership some former members who had dissented and to pray for an increase in the number of ministers, for the improvement of members' talents, for the continuation of peace and liberty, for divine aid for a member in trouble, and for blessings upon the church's efforts.[16]

The English Baptist pattern of holding days for prayer and fasting spread to America. When Elias Keach and others were prepared to organize the Pennepack Church in Pennsylvania in 1688, "a day was set apart to seek God by fasting and prayer in order to form ourselves into a Church state."[17] In 1787 the Grassy Creek Church in North Carolina used fasting and prayer upon ordaining a minister.[18] In 1803 the Black Creek Church in South Carolina employed this practice in ordaining deacons.[19] In 1871 the Mattaponi Church in Virginia held a day of prayer and fasting to pray for an increase in the number of ministers in its association.[20] By the end of the 1800s, special days for prayer and fasting existed in Baptist churches all across the country.

Associations in America in the 1700s and 1800s commonly recommended that their churches appoint special days for prayer and fasting. The Philadelphia Association made such a recommendation as early as 1726. Throughout the remainder of the 1700s, this important association proposed many days of prayer and fasting. Of these many events, five typical ones were designed to pray for more ministers (1732), for God's mercy in view of "the imminent danger our continent seems actually to labor under" (1754), for "the awful declension of religion in these middle States, and our national distresses" (1780), for relief from an epidemic and a drought (1793), and for "abounding error, infidelity, lukewarmness, and decay of vital piety" (1795).[21]

New England Baptist associations also encouraged days of prayer and fasting. In 1774 the Warren Association in Rhode Island approved four such days to be observed in 1775 because "our civil rights are invaded, and our religious privileges are also in danger."[22] The Woodstock Association in Vermont and the Bowdoinham Association in Maine also recommended such days in the late 1700s.

Examples of associations in the South which employed days of prayer and fasting in the 1700s and/or the early 1800s are the Sandy Creek, which included churches in North Carolina, South Carolina, and Virginia; the Kehukee in North Carolina; the Elkhorn and Salem, in Kentucky; the Dover, Ketocton, Portsmouth, Roanoke, and Strawberry, in Virginia; the Bethel, Charleston, and Edgefield, in South Carolina; the Georgia and Hephzibah, in Georgia; and the Cahawba and Muscle Shoal, in Alabama. The practice moved across the American frontier and into the West. The

Willamette Association in Oregon, for example, used the practice in the late 1850s. In all these cases, the purposes of days of prayer and fasting were similar to the purposes which Baptists had traditionally assigned to them.

Not only have associations suggested days of prayer and fasting for their churches but so have larger Baptist bodies. The General Assembly of the General Baptists in England proposed the practice throughout the 1700s, as did the General Conference of the Freewill Baptist Connection in the United States in the 1830s, 1840s, and 1850s. In 1867 the Southern Baptist Convention recommended to its churches "a day of fasting, humiliation and prayer, on account of the distressed condition of the country."[23] In the twentieth century, both the Southern Baptist Convention and the Northern Baptist Convention (renamed American Baptist Convention in 1950 and American Baptist Churches in the U.S.A. in 1972) continued to recommend special days of prayer. However, they mentioned fasting only occasionally.

The question to be raised now is, Considering the significance of fasting to the prayer life of Baptists for most of their history, why have special days for prayer and fasting declined dramatically among Baptists in the United States in the twentieth century? Four possible factors may account for this development.

First, as regular weekly prayer meetings began to take hold in Baptist life, special days for prayer and fasting may have declined for the same reason that monthly and quarterly prayer meetings did, namely, there was simply less need for them.

Second, as urbanization became an increasingly pronounced feature of American life and as working patterns changed, Baptists found it more difficult to take a full day off from work during the week to devote to prayer, fasting, and related events.

Third, with the multiplication of various kinds of prayer

meetings by churches and by women, youth, Sunday School supporters, and other groups within churches, most of which did not employ fasting, Baptists may gradually have taken the position that fasting was not as essential to effective prayer as once thought.

Fourth, fasting began to decline among Baptists almost simultaneously with the decline of two other important practices—the use of church covenants and church discipline. Thus, fasting may have been just one more victim of a general secularizing process which crept into Baptist life and neutralized the need for certain spiritual disciplines.

Approaches to Cultivating Prayer

Besides observing days of prayer and fasting, Baptists have also sponsored a wide range of other prayer emphases. Baptists have characteristically made prayer the foundation of their most significant achievements.

Missions

Baptists have probably created more special prayer emphases in behalf of missions than for any other cause. Perhaps the most important development in this regard for the Southern Baptist Convention was the formation in 1888 of Woman's Missionary Union (WMU) in an auxiliary relationship to the Convention. WMU promoted a day of prayer for foreign missions from 1888 through 1891. The emphasis became an entire week in 1892 (the centennial of the founding of the modern mission movement among Baptists by William Carey and Andrew Fuller) and has continued annually to the present as the Week of Prayer for Foreign Missions. The week was moved from January to December in 1926. WMU has also sponsored an annual Week of Prayer for Home Missions since 1895, although the name of the week varied in early years. The first week of March is set aside for this observance by churches. Both weeks of prayer were simply observances of WMU and its church organizations until 1957. In that year, they became churchwide observances.[24] Both observances are major annual events in most Southern Baptist churches.

During its history, WMU has also encouraged prayer for missions through many of the expressions of prayer mentioned at the beginning of this chapter. Through literature, special meetings, and missions organizations in churches, WMU has supported missions. Prayer mates (member of a missions organization becomes a prayer mate with a missionary) and the Season of Prayer for State Missions in September are other means used by WMU. (Of interest is the fact that the state WMU in one state, Virginia, had a Season of Prayer for State Missions as early as 1902.)[25]

WMU has performed a big service to Southern Baptists in promoting prayer support for Bold Mission Thrust, the effort of Southern Baptists to share the gospel with every person in the world by the year 2000. In 1977, when Bold Mission Thrust was in its formative stages, the Southern Baptist Convention adopted a three-point motion to designate the Sunday prior to each Convention meeting in 1978 and 1979 as a Day of Prayer for Bold Mission Thrust in churches, to conduct a prayer meeting for Bold Mission Thrust at some time during both annual meetings, and to request appropriate Convention agencies to develop guidelines for the day of prayer in the churches.[26]

The WMU accepted various opportunities to undergird Bold Mission Thrust with prayer support. In 1980 WMU initiated "Missions Pray-ers," a mission support team comprised of the homebound who engaged in a worldwide prayer ministry for Southern Baptist missions.[27]

In 1982 WMU and the Brotherhood Commission of the Southern Baptist Convention, an agency which has traditionally supported prayer for missions by Baptist men and boys, jointly published a twelve-page "Missions Prayer

Plan" in behalf of Bold Mission Thrust. Designed to continue for one year, beginning in October 1982, the purpose of the plan was "to lead the entire church to pray specifically and intelligently for Southern Baptist missions, that the world may believe."[28] The plan included a prayer calendar, action plans, resources, a list of specific mission needs for which to pray, suggested ways to pray, and other helps.

In various publications, such as *World Mission Journal, Baptist Men's Handbook,* and *Baptist Men's Support Guide,* the Brotherhood Commission has encouraged men's prayer groups, prayer retreats, prayer diaries, and other means of enhancing the prayer life of men and boys. In addition to its publications, another approach which the Brotherhood Commission has used to involve men in praying for missions has been regional and national prayer breakfasts. For example, the agency sponsored a national prayer breakfast in Atlanta, Georgia, in 1973, another in Dallas, Texas, in 1974, and sixteen vocational prayer breakfasts in 1978 in Atlanta.[29]

Other agencies of the Southern Baptist Convention have also developed special ways to promote missions through prayer. Three examples are The Sunday School Board, the Foreign Mission Board, and the Home Mission Board. All three have used periodicals, such as *Home Life, The Commission,* and *Missions USA,* to present prayer strategies. For several years, the Foreign Mission Board has even had a staff position devoted to coordinating intercessory prayer for missions. A major emphasis of this position is to get the prayer needs of foreign missionaries to Southern Baptists willing to pray.[30] In 1983 the Home Mission Board initiated an Intercessory Prayer Line which enabled Southern Baptists nationwide to call the board toll free "to learn of home mission needs and requests for prayer" and for the board's missionaries to call "to request prayer for their work and concerns."[31] The telephone number was 1-800-554-PRAY. (By 1982 the Canadian Baptist Overseas Mission Board had in place a prayer line on which Baptists all across Canada could place a call using the number 1-416-920-PRAY and hear a one-minute recorded message which briefed them on urgent prayer requests of missionaries overseas.)[32]

The Southern Baptist Convention as a body has supported a variety of prayer efforts for missions. The Baptist Jubilee Advance was a five-year (1959-1964) program with annual emphases celebrating the 150th anniversary of the rise of the first national body of Baptists in America—the Triennial Convention, formed in 1814. The Southern Baptist Convention voted to urge its churches "to conduct or participate in watch-night prayer services, December 31, 1962, for the 1963 Baptist Jubilee Emphasis on World Missions."[33]

Another Baptist convention which actively advanced special prayer emphases for missions was the Northern Baptist Convention. In 1908, because of the serious financial needs of its missionary societies and enterprises, the convention passed a resolution requesting the officers of its societies to unite in calling Northern Baptists "to observe a week of prayer to definitely spread these great needs before the God of missions, and to seek the divine guidance to meet these needs and deliverance from these perils."[34] In 1922 a convention report recommended for 1922-1923 the use of a "Cycle of Prayer" every month by every member of every church to undergird the denomination's missionary enterprise. The cycle listed specific items to be prayed for each day of the month.[35] In 1925, because missionaries were reporting cases of answered prayer on mission fields as a result of a special denominational day of prayer for the work, the Foreign Mission Society reported that it had printed a leaflet entitled "Answered Prayers in the Orient."[36]

In 1933 the Northern Baptist Convention's Board of Missionary Cooperation reported on the "Pray It Through" movement which the board had begun to improve receipts for missions. The goal was to form a prayer band of Baptists around the world. Within the first year, about 400,000 prayer cards were printed, prayer calendars were being printed at the rate of 200,000 a month, and the board's "Pray It Through" poster was one of the most widely used posters ever distributed by the denomination up to that time.[37]

American Baptists (formerly Northern Baptists) have continued through the years to promote prayer for missions in creative ways. In 1984 the American Baptist Churches in the U.S.A., along with ten other North American Baptist bodies, including Woman's Missionary Union, Auxiliary to the Southern Baptist Convention, sponsored a national Baptist Prayer Conference in Columbus, Ohio, which focused on many issues, one of which was missions.[38]

Evangelism and Revivalism

C. E. Autrey, a Baptist professor of evangelism, described prayer in an important textbook on evangelism as essential to evangelistic visitation and to revivalism. He believed that helpful preparation for revival could include individual prayer, neighborhood prayer meetings, all-day prayer meetings of the church, special periods of prayer during the revival effort, and an all-night prayer meeting in the middle of a revival.[39] Autrey's suggestions contributed to a long list of attempts in Baptist life to relate prayer to evangelism and revivalism.

In the twentieth century, Baptists have often established this relationship through convention resolutions. For example, the 1937 Southern Baptist Convention recognized the need for a spiritual awakening, affirming that "all spiritual awakenings come as a result of earnest, fervent, believing prayer," and acknowledging that their Home Mission Board had just revived its Department of Evangelism. The messengers resolved to "endorse a Convention-wide prayer-covenant" to surrender their lives more completely to Christ through prayer and evangelistic witness so that a worldwide revival might result.[40] Daily hours to pray were suggested for each time zone across the country.

In 1955 and 1956, adopted reports of the Committee on Resolutions of the American Baptist Convention urged churches to engage in special prayer ministries for evangelism.[41]

The Southern Baptist Convention's 1970 resolution "On Evangelism and Prayer" requested Convention officers to ask President Richard Nixon to set aside two days of prayer in July for spiritual awakening in the nation; requested the officers to ask the Baptist World Alliance meeting in Tokyo, Japan, in July to set aside a prayer time for worldwide revival; and asked churches to set aside a twenty-four-hour prayer period in July to pray for revival in the nation.[42]

Evangelistic crusades have also elicited prayer responses from Baptists. Three examples from the 1960s can help show this. In 1963 Joseph B. Underwood, consultant for evangelism and church development for the Southern Baptist Foreign Mission Board, issued an appeal for prayer in behalf of simultaneous evangelistic crusades to take place among the English-speaking Baptist churches and missions of Europe in September of that year.[43]

In 1966 several Baptist churches in France held a week of prayer to pray for a nationwide evangelistic campaign to be held in 1967 in the French Baptist Federation.[44]

The Crusade of the Americas, an evangelistic crusade in 1968-1969 involving twenty million Baptists in North, South, and Central America, led to several major prayer challenges. Baptist men were to lead in observing the Hemispheric Day of Prayer on the second Sunday of each year of the crusade. The Baptist World Alliance designated these same days as worldwide days of prayer for the crusade.[45] At the request of the Southern Baptist Convention, Woman's Missionary Union (with promotional and financial assistance from the Convention's mission boards) organized

PACT. As an international prayer plan designed to support the Crusade of the Americas, "PACT linked individuals, churches, church organizations, and families in intercession for the crusade."[46] The distribution of over 1,120,600 fliers in English, Spanish, and Portuguese, plus other promotion, resulted in requests for prayer partners from forty-nine states and twenty-nine countries.[47]

A key development in the Evangelism Section of the Southern Baptist Home Mission Board was the existence by 1981 of a program entitled "Spiritual Awakening" and a staff position entitled "special assistant in spiritual awakening." Program objectives were "to facilitate spiritual awakening among Southern Baptists" and "to help churches through their associations and state conventions develop spiritual awakening events and processes."[48] The program has focused heavily on prayer events. For example, in 1981 it coordinated the first National Conference on Prayer for Spiritual Awakening at Ridgecrest, North Carolina; in 1982 it sponsored a second conference with the same title at Glorieta, New Mexico.[49] By 1981 the program included for churches and associations an eight-hour "Prayer for Spiritual Awakening Seminar" which could be used on a weekend retreat or in an in-church prayer emphasis. Certified seminar instructors used a special packet of leadership materials and the film, *The Role of Prayer in Spiritual Awakening*.[50]

In an especially significant meeting in 1983, Southern Baptist state evangelism directors launched plans for simultaneous revivals to occur in 28,000 Southern Baptist churches in 1986. During the opening address of the meeting, Robert Hamblin, evangelism vice-president of the Home Mission Board, urged the directors to promote 1985 as a year of prayer in preparation for the 1986 revivals.[51]

Cooperative Relationships

The Baptist World Alliance has sponsored special international days of prayer for Baptist women, men, and youth. The Women's Department of the Alliance took the first step by launching the Baptist Women's Day of Prayer in 1950. This action resulted from a 1948 suggestion of the European Baptist Women's Union to hold a day of prayer to further reconciliation in war-torn Europe. In 1963 the date was changed from the first Friday in December to the first Monday in November. In 1980 the Women's Department renamed the day the Baptist Women's World Day of Prayer. The day has been observed on every continent.[52] Examination of monthly issues (published since the early 1960s) of *The Baptist World,* publication of the Baptist World Alliance, and of news releases of *Baptist Press* and the *European Baptist Press Service* revealed numerous announcements about and reports from observances of the day from countries all around the world. A 1979 announcement expected the day to attract up to one million women "to thousands of prayer centers in a hundred nations" for that year's observance.[53]

In describing the meaning of this special day of prayer for women, Mrs. Edgar Bates, president of the Women's Department of the Alliance in 1965, claimed that it provided a sense of "oneness and wholeness" among women as they recommitted themselves to God. "What a wonderful thing," she wrote, ". . . in the face of all the differences that exist among Baptist women brought about by distances, different nationalities, racial backgrounds, degrees of education, cultural ideals, that we are able to find oneness in prayer."[54]

The Men's Department of the Baptist World Alliance has sponsored the Baptist Men's Worldwide Day of Witness and Prayer since 1976. The recommended date in that year was the fourth Monday in February, but it has been the fourth Saturday in April since 1977. The Men's Department annually develops a special program for the day and promotes it through the distribution of literature. Men around the world are typically encouraged to pray for one another, for the work of the Alliance, and for people and causes presented in specific prayer requests. The Men's Department has also invited men to consider establishing continuing prayer groups of laymen to join together and pray on a weekly, monthly, or quarterly basis for spiritual awakening.[55]

By 1983 the Youth Department of the Baptist World Alliance was promoting a Baptist Youth Day of Prayer. The designated day for that year was the second Sunday in June. Elaborate planning and special meetings were not suggested to churches. Instead, the Youth Department simply asked each Baptist church in every country to have a special prayer for global efforts in youth ministry. The purpose of the day was "to unite all Baptist youth in prayer concern."[56]

Peace and Other Ethical Concerns

Peace has been a perennial concern of Baptist prayer life. The Baptist World Alliance, Baptist conventions and unions, denominational agencies, churches, and other Baptist bodies have created special prayer emphases in behalf of peace. Developments in Baptist life since the early 1940s illustrate this point well.

The Baptist World Alliance and its Congresses have aggressively promoted prayer for peace. In 1950 the Eighth Baptist World Congress commended to all Baptists the importance of praying for peace in Korea. In 1956 the Alliance's Administrative Committee urged prayer for peace in Hungary. In 1972 V. Carney Hargroves, Alliance president, issued a call to prayer for conferences about to occur between leaders of the United States and those of Peking and Moscow. In 1973 an Alliance administrative subcommittee endorsed a request of twenty-one missionaries in Israel to designate December 23 as a World Day of Prayer for peace in the Middle East. In 1977 a major development took place when the Alliance established an annual World Day of Prayer for Peace to be held on the Sunday in October preceding the anniversary of the founding of the United Nations (formed October 24, 1945).[57]

Baptist conventions and unions have also made important appeals for prayers for peace. During World War II, the Northern Baptist Convention encouraged its churches to seek peace by using one or both of two prayer plans being promoted—"America's Prayer Minute" and an effort to enroll "Millions of Intercessors."[58] In 1944 the Southern Baptist Convention adopted a special committee report entitled "Southern Baptists and World Peace" which asked Southern Baptists to "pray that God may guide the nations of the world into a righteous and enduring peace."[59] In 1948 the Northern Baptist Convention joined the Christians of Japan in designating August 6 as "a day for repentance and prayer for peace," remembering that on that day in 1945 the first atomic bomb used in actual warfare had been dropped on Hiroshima, Japan.[60]

The 1956 adopted report of the Committee on Resolutions of the American Baptist Convention included a section on "Prayers for Peace." It reaffirmed belief in prayer as an instrument for world peace, commended churches for stimulating the growth of prayer groups, and also commended people of those countries willing to cooperate in prayer for world peace. The 1957 convention again approved these same prayer statements.[61]

Regarding the Vietnam War, the Japan Baptist Convention initiated a special prayer movement for world peace in 1967. In 1972 the Baptist Union of Sweden urged its churches to devote portions of worship services to prayer for peace in Indochina.[62]

In the early 1980s, a group concerned for world peace at

the Deer Park Baptist Church in Louisville, Kentucky, formed a new publication, *Baptist Peacemaker*. The group has sponsored a number of events which have stressed prayer for peace. Samplings from 1982 illustrate this point. In January of that year, E. Glenn Hinson, noted Southern Baptist church historian, published a cover-page article in the *Baptist Peacemaker* entitled "Hopeful Happenings for Peace." He devoted several paragraphs to the urgency and value of praying for peace. In May 1982 the Louisville group announced that it would sponsor six prayer meetings for world peace during the June Southern Baptist Convention meeting in New Orleans, Louisiana. In August the group sponsored in Louisville a National Peace Convocation entitled "Strategies for Peacemaking" on the thirty-seventh anniversary of the atomic bombing of Hiroshima, Japan. The three-day convocation included five workshops, one of which dealt with "Prayer and Peacemaking."[63]

The Christian Life Commission of the Southern Baptist Convention has the world peace emphasis as a program assignment from the Convention. Thus, after the 1983 Convention approved the idea of an annual Day of Prayer for World Peace and placed it on the denominational calendar for the first Sunday in August, the Christian Life Commission soon approved the development of resources to support the first such day to be held on August 5, 1984. The agency prepared a twelve-page "Planning Guide" for the special day which described its purpose, offered suggestions for observing it through worship and a prayer vigil, presented ways to build continuous involvement for peace with justice, included Bible studies relating to peace and prayer, and listed other resources available from the agency which could be useful for the emphasis. Each year the agency develops a theme for the day and prepares support materials, and the Baptist Bulletin Service has a special bulletin cover for the day.[64]

Besides peace, Baptists have focused special prayer emphases upon other ethical issues as well. A few examples may help. Walter Rauschenbusch, Baptist leader of the Social Gospel Movement in the early 1900s, claimed that "if we had more prayer in common on the sins of modern society, there would be more social repentance and less angry resistance to the demands of justice and mercy."[65]

In 1956 Joseph H. Jackson, president of the National Baptist Convention, Inc., announced a day of prayer and fasting for May 17, 1956, the second anniversary of the Supreme Court decision requiring desegregation of public schools. The purpose was to seek God's forgiveness for the way Americans were sinning against one another's rights.[66]

In 1964 the Baptist General Convention of Texas approved the recommendation of its Christian Life Commission to "set aside Sunday, January 10, 1965, as a Special Day of Prayer concerning the moral issue of legalized gambling in our state."[67]

In 1969 the president and general secretary of the Baptist Union of Ireland prepared and distributed a call to prayer and repentance to the Union's eighty churches with a request that their appeal be read at two successive Sunday morning services during November. The appeal acknowledged "the continuing spiritual, social, and political sickness which afflicts Northern Ireland" and then urged "every Irish Baptist to repent every day before God of any injustice, intolerance, and suspicion that may be in our hearts towards our fellow-citizens whatever their religious creed or political complexion, and to ask His forgiveness."[68]

Convention Meetings

Throughout their history Baptists have designated special prayer emphases for convention meetings. In 1814, the year of its formation, the Triennial Convention, the first national body of Baptists in America, established a prayer meeting to implore the direction and blessing of the Holy Spirit upon its proceedings. In 1817 the Convention observed prayer meetings every morning at six o'clock during the sessions.[69]

The Southern Baptist Convention adopted a resolution in 1880 urging churches to use the Sunday preceding the 1881 Convention meeting "as an occasion of special prayer" for the deliberations of the Convention.[70] In the early 1930s, the Northern Baptist Convention regularly held prayer meetings during its sessions to seek God's guidance.[71]

More recently, special prayer efforts in behalf of Southern Baptist Convention meetings have become quite common. In 1981 under the direction of Jack R. Taylor, the Convention's first vice-president, a "Prayer Mobilization Plan" was implemented. The plan included the enlistment of a prayer coordinator in each state convention and fellowship, the designation of May 24 as a day of prayer throughout the Convention, and the setting aside of one prayer room in the Convention meeting facility and another in the Convention hotel.[72] Similar plans were implemented in 1982-1984 under the direction of the Convention's first vice-presidents.

Colleges and Seminaries

Baptists have developed many special prayer emphases both in behalf of and in the context of higher education, especially theological education. Several examples since 1975 can help to show the nature of some of these emphases.

On October 23, 1975, the Baptist Theological Seminary of Ruschlikon, Switzerland, observed a Day of Prayer for Seminaries in Europe.[73] In 1976 California Baptist College at Riverside founded a Chair of Discipleship, the first in the nation, around which an academic minor was developed with courses covering the disciplines of Christian growth, one of which was prayer.[74] In 1979 The Southern Baptist Theological Seminary in Louisville, Kentucky, established the endowed Ellen Edens McCall Chair of Prayer and Personal Devotion.[75] In 1984 Southwestern Baptist Theological Seminary in Fort Worth, Texas, set up the endowed Chair of Prayer and Spiritual Formation.[76] The "Prayer Calendar" of the Canadian Baptist Federation for the last quarter of 1984 suggested October 7-13 as days of special prayer for Baptist educational institutions across Canada.[77]

Other Special Emphases

At times Baptists have used special prayer efforts in behalf of many other important areas of their life. Three such areas are stewardship, the family, and local church prayer ministries. Regarding stewardship, the 1960 Southern Baptist Convention, for example, voted to urge every Southern Baptist church "to conduct or participate in Watch-night Prayer Services, December 31, 1960, for our 1961 Baptist Jubilee Emphasis on Stewardship and Enlistment."[78] Further, on May 13, 1975, the Stewardship Commission of the Convention sponsored a Cooperative Program Prayer Breakfast in Memphis, Tennessee. In 1925 the Convention had adopted the Cooperative Program, the Southern Baptist method of denominational finance, in Memphis.[79]

Regarding the family, the 1982-1985 Bold Mission Thrust Program Emphasis of the Southern Baptist Convention included a goal by 1985 of having "500,000 family units committed to family worship and Bible study in the home."[80] In 1985-1986 the Family Ministry Department of the Southern Baptist Sunday School Board promoted a special focus on discipleship in the home which highlighted prayer.[81]

Concerning local church prayer ministries, one pattern in a few churches within the last decade has been to create staff positions relating to prayer. For example, in 1977 the Southcliff Baptist Church in Fort Worth, Texas, employed Richard L. Shepherd as Associate Pastor in Prayer Ministries. Another trend has been for churches to develop regular or periodic prayer ministries, such as prayer seminars, days of prayer,

prayer retreats, special prayer meetings, prayer fellowships for families, and practical written aids to prayer. Attention has also focused on the formation of intercessory prayer ministries. The Cottage Hill Baptist Church in Mobile, Alabama, as illustration, developed an around-the-clock, seven-day-a-week intercessory prayer chain in 1974 which was still continuing in 1984.[82]

Conclusion

Baptists have created special prayer emphases for centuries. These emphases have varied in nature, purpose, longevity, and value. Primary contributions of the emphases have been to magnify prayer in Baptist life and to relate prayer closely to the major concerns of Baptists. Through the dynamic application of prayer to personal, family, and corporate needs, Baptists have made prayer an integrating discipline of their faith.

During their first three hundred years, Baptists commonly appointed special days for prayer and fasting. They used these occasions to prepare for the Lord's Supper, to ordain church officers, to confess sin and seek forgiveness, to solicit God's blessings, to secure relief from difficult situations, to discipline errant church members, to ask God to provide more ministers, to entreat revival, and to achieve other goals.

Special days for prayer and fasting have declined significantly in the twentieth century. Contributing factors have included the rise of regular weekly prayer meetings in churches, an increase in urbanization and changes in working patterns, the multiplication of various kinds of prayer meetings, and a general secularizing process which has entered Baptist life.

C. H. Spurgeon wrote, "The church of God would be far stronger to wrestle with this ungodly age if she were more given to prayer and fasting. There is a mighty efficacy in these two gospel ordinances. The first links us to heaven, the second separates us from earth."[83] What response should contemporary Baptists give to these claims, considering the importance of the joint practice of prayer and fasting in such a large portion of the Baptist heritage?

Baptists have typically cultivated special approaches to prayer in such vital areas as missions, evangelism, and revivalism; cooperative relationships, peace, and other ethical concerns; convention meetings, colleges, and seminaries; and stewardship, family life, and local church prayer ministries. These approaches have taken the form of special publications, recommended times and settings for prayer, guidelines for developing prayer ministries, and other helps.

Special emphases have added depth and quality to the prayer life of Baptists. Many have been designed to be one-time events, but others have had impact year after year. An example of the latter is the Week of Prayer for Foreign Missions which has been flourishing among Southern Baptists since 1892. New prayer emphases are still emerging, as reflected in the first Day of Prayer for World Peace among Southern Baptists in 1984.

Viewed as a whole, the special prayer emphases of Baptists say some important things about Baptist concepts of prayer. Prayer relates to all of life. Cultivation of prayer requires constant attention. Prayer is a form of communion with God which can lead to dynamic growth in denominational enterprises. Commitment to God through special prayer emphases has been and must continue to be a fundamental feature of the prayer story of Baptists.

4

Prayer and Freedom

Baptists love freedom. They choose the freedom of salvation, not the bondage of sin. They believe in the priesthood of the believer, not in an earthly high priest. They write confessions of faith, not creeds. They support individual interpretation of the Bible, not papal pronouncements. They cherish religious liberty, not spiritual coercion. They advocate separation of church and state, not a state church. They prefer local church government, not episcopal control. Voluntarism in the context of responsibility is basic to Baptist life.

Baptist views of freedom perhaps reach their highest point of significance in the practice of prayer. To commune with God is the ultimate privilege available to God's people. In prayer true freedom becomes real as God offers forgiveness for sin, healing for sickness, peace for anxiety, direction for aimlessness, meaning for despair, relationship for loneliness, and justice for inequity.

Baptists look to Christ as their model in prayer. They turn the pages of the entire Bible for inspiration from the prayer life of the saints. Their own denominational heritage offers them a deep reservoir of experience in prayer. In recent years they have engaged vigorously in the debate about prayer in public schools. Baptists' attention to prayer in the Bible, church history, and current debate vividly illustrates the close connection they make between prayer and freedom.

Prayer and Freedom in the Bible

The Bible reveals various relationships between prayer and freedom. Perhaps the most obvious relationship exists in situations in which biblical persons prayed for freedom from limitations upon their own lives and/or the lives of others. Such situations with a few illustrations of each include prayers for freedom from:

Physical Illness.—David prayed for his sick child (2 Sam. 12:16); a man of God prayed for Jeroboam's withered hand (1 Kings 13:6); Hezekiah prayed for personal healing (2 Kings 20:3); Paul prayed for the father of Publius who had fever and dysentery (Acts 28:8); and Paul stated that he had prayed three times about a thorn in his own flesh (2 Cor. 12:8).

Death.—Elijah prayed for the resurrection of a widow's son (1 Kings 17:21); Elisha, for the resurrection of a Shunammite woman's son (2 Kings 4:33); and Peter, for the resurrection of Dorcas (Acts 9:40).

Barrenness.—Isaac prayed that his barren wife, Rebekah, would be able to conceive (Gen. 25:21); Hannah prayed that God would replace her childlessness with a son whom she could devote to the Lord (1 Sam. 1:11); and an angel announced to Zechariah that, in response to his prayer, he and his barren wife, Elizabeth, were to become the parents of John (Luke 1:13).

Sin.—Examples of people in the Bible who sought freedom from sin through confession in prayer either for themselves or for the people of God are David (2 Sam. 24:10), Ezra (Ezra 10:1), Nehemiah (Neh. 1:6), Jeremiah (Jer. 14:7), Daniel (Dan. 9:4-5), and the tax-collector in a parable of Jesus (Luke 18:13). Jesus taught His disciples to seek forgiveness for debts through prayer (Matt. 6:12).

Bondage and Distress.—The Israelites prayed for release from Egyptian bondage (Ex. 2:23); Hezekiah, for freedom from

Assyrian captivity (2 Kings 19:15-19); and Asa, for help against Ethiopian attack (2 Chron. 14:11). The psalmist urged the redeemed of the Lord to thank God through prayer for the freedom He had given them from such distresses as hunger, thirst, imprisonment, sickness, and storms at sea (Ps. 107). Jeremiah sought relief through prayer from his perplexity about the way the wicked seemed to prosper in the presence of a righteous God (Jer. 12:1). Jonah prayed for deliverance from the belly of a fish (Jonah 2). Jesus prayed for freedom from His forthcoming persecution, but in the context of complete obedience to His Father's will (Matt. 26:39). Paul encouraged the Philippians to find peace from anxiety through communion with God (Phil. 4:6).

A second type of relationship between prayer and freedom in the Bible is that of praying for personal freedom and strength to do God's will. The prayer life of Jesus clearly illustrates this relationship. Jesus' prayer at the time of His baptism represents His free and total commitment to His Father and to His Father's mission for Him (Luke 3:21). In the liberty of prayer, Jesus taught His disciples to pray for God's kingdom to come and His will to be done (Matt. 6:10). The frequent prayers of Jesus in the wilderness, in the hills, on a mountain, and in other places show His desire to live freely and fully in His Father's purpose (Luke 5:16; 6:12; 9:18,28; 11:1). John 17 is a long prayer of Jesus in which He asked the Father to glorify the Son who in freedom was sharing the Father's gift of eternal life with all who would hear in the hope that they would receive it and freely share it with others. And, of course, Jesus' prayers in Gethsemane (Matt. 26:39) and on the cross (Luke 23:46) depict the extent to which He was willing to use His freedom in obedience to His Father.

A third type of relationship between prayer and freedom in the Bible exists in the persecution of the people of God. Religious and governmental officials who placed God's people in a lions' den or imprisoned them or stoned them or in other ways persecuted them discovered that they could not restrict the freedom of those people to pray. Ironically, bodily persecution, which is designed to destroy all freedom, cultivates one of the truest expressions of freedom, the right to commune with God.

An excellent Old Testament illustration appears in Daniel 6. Out of jealousy for the plan of King Darius to make Daniel, an exile from Judah, the chief administrator of his kingdom, numerous officials under Darius devised a strategy intended to abolish that plan. They pressured Darius to accept their agreement that the king pass and enforce an ordinance to throw into a den of lions anyone who prayed within thirty days to any god or man, except to Darius himself. Darius signed a document approving this law.

Daniel boldly refused to let governmental decree dictate the nature of his prayer life. Upon hearing that the king had established the new regulation, Daniel followed his normal practice of free prayer by going to an upper room in his house, falling to his knees, and praying to God three times a day. Observing Daniel in prayer to God, the men attempting to frame him convinced the king to command that Daniel be tossed into a den of lions. The king issued such a command, but God protected Daniel from personal harm because of Daniel's prayerful trust in his Father. Daniel's experience shows that no outside force can destroy one's freedom to pray and that one's prayer life can reveal the true nature of God's support and thereby free a person to rise above potentially destructive situations.

New Testament persecutions intended to destroy Jesus and His followers were not able to destroy their prayer life and, in fact, led them to new levels of freedom in prayer. While hanging on the cross, Jesus, in an ultimate surge of freedom, victoriously asked His Father's forgiveness for His persecutors (Luke 23:34) and committed His spirit into His Father's hands (v. 46).

The early church, as described in Acts, was full of Christians who experienced the deepest possible freedom through prayer in times of enormous suffering. Consider four examples.

- In response to the charge of the Sanhedrin, or supreme court, that they were not to speak or teach any more in the name of Jesus (4:18), and in response to additional threats from this body (v. 21), Peter and John resorted to prayer and asked God to intensify their boldness to speak His word faithfully (v. 29).
- Stephen, victimized by the rage of his opponents who threw him out of Jerusalem and stoned him because of his resolute commitment to Christ, soared to seldom reached heights of freedom during the stoning by praying for Jesus to receive his spirit and to forgive his persecutors (7:59-60).
- Herod placed Peter in prison; the church prayed earnestly for Peter; and an angel of the Lord freed Peter from prison (12:1-11).
- Imprisoned in Philippi, Paul and Silas prayed and sang hymns at midnight. A great earthquake suddenly shook open the doors of the prison and unfastened the fetters of all the prisoners (16:25-26). Paul and Silas used their freedom to prevent the jailer from committing suicide, to present the salvation of Jesus Christ to him, and to baptize him and all his family (vv. 27-33).

Prayer and Freedom in the Baptist Story

Baptists emerged into history as a people in search of freedom, and prayer was a vital part of the search. Early Baptists in England and America faced considerable persecution. Through it all, prayer sustained the faithful. In the early 1600s, King James I of England, after whom the King James Version of the Bible was named, placed in prison

Thomas Helwys, the first Baptist pastor on English soil. Imprisoned because of his bold defense of religious freedom, Helwys died before his release. Roger Williams fled the oppressive religious authorities of New England to establish a haven of religious liberty at Providence Plantation in Rhode Island. There he became the first pastor of the first Baptist church in America in 1638/39. The prayer experiences of Helwys, Williams, and other early Baptists helped to form a dynamic denomination of freedom-loving Christians.

Now let's shift to Virginia. The setting is a cell in Urbanna Prison in Middlesex County. The date is August 12, 1771. John Waller is writing a letter to a fellow Baptist. One of at least thirty Virginia Baptist ministers imprisoned, whipped, or stoned between 1768 and 1777 in a head-on collision between Baptists and the Church of England, Waller describes how he and several companions were jailed for preaching without licenses. In an appeal for prayer, he then concludes: "We cannot tell how long we shall be kept in bonds; we therefore beseech, dear brother, that you and the church supplicate night and day for us, our benefactors and our persecutors."[1]

Threats also confronted Baptists in New England in the late 1700s. The Warren Baptist Association suggested the following to its churches in its 1774 circular letter: "And as it is a day of great affliction, when our civil rights are invaded, and our religious privileges also in danger, we . . . recommend to you four days in . . . the ensuing year for fasting and prayer."[2] The days suggested were the Fridays before the last Sundays in November, February, May, and August.

From colonial America, shift to the modern world, remembering along the way both the atrocities committed upon black Baptists during the era of slavery and the freedom-oriented spirituals which they prayerfully sang with intense meaning. Baptists today continue to suffer infringements upon their freedom, and prayer continues as a vital response to such oppression. A few illustrations will show the relationship between such infringements and prayer.

Because of increasing attacks upon the religious freedom of evangelical Christians in Spain in the late 1950s, H. Cornell Goerner, an area secretary for the Southern Baptist Foreign Mission Board, urged all Baptists to join in a worldwide day of prayer that the injustices might be eliminated.[3]

Baptist churches in the Republic of Congo observed a day of prayer in 1962 for 200,000 Angolan refugees in Lower Congo, 10,000 of whom were Baptists.[4]

A 1965 report revealed that Herbert Caudill and James David Fite, two Southern Baptist missionaries imprisoned in Cuba because of sentences imposed by the Castro government, were daily conducting prayer meetings in their cell block for fellow prisoners who wished to participate.[5]

In 1972 leaders of the French Baptist Federation issued a call to prayer for large numbers of Baptist refugees leaving the Central African republic of Burundi to escape persecution, which had already claimed the lives of eleven of the fourteen members of the executive committee of the Burundi Baptist churches.[6]

The relationship between prayer and freedom in recent Baptist life achieved a unique significance in the experiences of a noted black Baptist preacher who sacrificed his life in the name of civil and religious freedom. As an important study of the prayer tradition of blacks pointed out, "The liberating relevance of the Black prayer tradition reached its modern-day summit in the heroic life and philosophy of Martin Luther King, Jr. During the days of his leadership, prayer was an integral part of every struggle, meeting, and decision."[7]

Consider the experience of Georgi Vins, a Soviet Baptist pastor. "Bumping across Siberia in a cattle car" a few days before his release on April 27, 1979, from years of sufferings and harsh Soviet imprisonment, Vins worshiped two days later in the First Baptist Church of Washington, D. C. There in a moving testimony of faith, he began his benediction to the morning service, using an interpreter, as follows: "Almighty Lord, I bring you my sincere gratitude for this moment, for your strength, for the miracle you have shown in our life."[8] Prayer and freedom coexisted in victorious celebration.

As the largest Protestant denomination in the United States, the Southern Baptist Convention has passed many resolutions relating to prayer and freedom. Three examples occurred in the early to mid-1970s. A 1971 resolution "On Voluntary Prayer" affirmed that no prayer is genuine unless it is voluntary and that prayer "must be kept free from governmental or ecclesiastical intrusion."[9] A 1974 resolution "On Prayer for Persecuted Christians" called for Southern Baptists to pray for all Christians in the world "who are being persecuted because they are believers in Jesus Christ."[10] A 1975 resolution "On Prayer for Religious Freedom" acknowledged continuing restraints on religious freedom in various parts of the world and expressed a renewed commitment "to pray and fast for these persecuted Christians."[11]

Prayer and Freedom in Public Schools

The religion clauses of the First Amendment in the Bill of Rights of the United States Constitution state: "Congress shall make no law respecting an establishment of religion, or prohibiting the free exercise thereof." The Fourteenth Amendment and decisions of the Supreme Court extended the prohibition of government authority in religion to all governments—state and local as well as federal.

Because infractions against the First Amendment did arise relating to prayer and Bible reading in public schools, the Supreme Court made two of its most important church-state decisions of the twentieth century in the early 1960s. On

June 25, 1962, in *Engel v. Vitale,* the Court ruled that the formulation of official or prescribed prayers by state authorities for use in public schools is unconstitutional. Official government prayers violated the establishment clause of the First Amendment. Then on June 17, 1963, in *Abingdon School District v. Schempp,* the Court ruled unconstitutional the practice of requiring Bible readings and the recitation of the Lord's Prayer in public schools.

Failure to understand the intent of the Supreme Court in these school prayer cases has led since 1962 to a steady stream of proposals introduced in Congress designed to amend the Constitution or achieve legislation which would, in effect, rescind the *Engel* and *Schempp* decisions. By 1981 almost two hundred such proposals had been introduced.[12]

On May 6, 1982, at a National Day of Prayer ceremony at the White House, President Ronald Reagan announced his intention to send to Congress his proposal for a constitutional amendment on prayer in public schools. The proposal read: "Nothing in this Constitution shall be construed to prohibit individual or group prayer in public schools or other public institutions. No person shall be required by the United States or by any state to participate in prayer." On July 12, 1983, Reagan indicated that he was sending to Congress a revised version of his proposal which added the following sentence: "Nor shall the United States or any state compose the words of any prayer to be said in public schools." On March 20, 1984, the United States Senate rejected Reagan's proposed constitutional amendment.

A Baptist church-state expert commented that the Senate defeat of Reagan's effort to restore state-sanctioned prayer in public schools "marks a new watershed and potential turning point in the long and bitter debate over the proper role of religion in public schools." He continued by claiming that the "voluntary" question was the key to the defeat: "Despite repeated claims by President Reagan that all he sought was a return to voluntary prayer, too many senators and citizens came to realize that in many, if not most instances, the prayers to be recited would have been anything but voluntary."[13]

Shortly after the defeat of President Reagan's proposed prayer amendment, the United States Senate passed an "equal access" measure in June 1984, and in July the House of Representatives did the same, thus clearing the measure for Reagan's signature. The Equal Access Act became law on August 11, 1984. This legislation requires "that secular and religious non-school-sponsored student groups be granted equal access to any limited open forum created in a public school when the students meet on their own initiative and without any official encouragement or sponsorship for religious discussion and prayer."[14]

Passage of the equal access measure "marked the first time Congress has cleared substantive legislation dealing with the role of religion in public schools since the landmark 1962-63 Supreme Court decisions on school prayer."[15] The equal access approach may offer the most promise for Americans seeking a legitimate presence of religion in public schools. It "seems the best alternative yet" for those desiring a healthy balance between the no establishment and the free exercise clauses of the First Amendment. And because of the decisive Senate defeat of President Reagan's proposed prayer amendment, "equal access may be the only realistic alternative for years to come."[16]

Selected Southern and State Baptist Convention Reactions

Both the Southern Baptist Convention and state conventions have generally expressed strong support for the 1962 and 1963 Supreme Court decisions and strong opposition to various proposed constitutional prayer amendments. In 1963 the Southern Baptist Convention adopted the report of its Public Affairs Committee which stated that the Baptist

Joint Committee on Public Affairs and its staff had taken official positions supporting the Supreme Court's 1962 prayer decision.[17] The Convention also approved the Public Affairs Committee's 1972 report which stated that on the basis of the Convention's adoption of its 1971 resolution "On Voluntary Prayer," the Baptist Joint Committee had successfully participated in an effort to prevent passage of a proposed prayer amendment in the United States House of Representatives.[18]

The 1980 Convention passed a resolution "On Voluntary Prayer in Public Schools." Affirming that the Supreme Court "has not held that it is illegal for any individual to pray or read his or her Bible in public schools," the Convention resolved both to oppose all attempts "to circumvent the Supreme Court's decisions forbidding government authored or sponsored religious exercises in public schools" and to affirm its belief "in the right to have voluntary prayer in the public schools."[19]

In response to the proposed prayer amendment of President Ronald Reagan, the 1982 Convention adopted a resolution "On Prayer in Schools" in which it declared its support for the amendment.[20] Commenting on this reversal of traditional position, E. Glenn Hinson, noted Southern Baptist church historian, claimed that approval of this resolution "ignore[d] more than 300 years of our history. In the past Southern Baptists repeatedly rejected that approach. To impose any kind of religious rites in public school is something that would have been abhorrent to our forebears."[21]

The 1984 Convention adopted a resolution "On Equal Access Legislation" which favored passage of an equal access bill being considered in Congress. The 1984 resolution supported the principle "that if a public school establishes a limited open forum consisting of non-school-sponsored, student-initiated, student-controlled, student group meetings, no such group may be excluded on the basis of the religious content of speech used in its meetings." The 1985 Convention approved a resolution "On Equal Access," urging Southern Baptists to understand and implement the Equal Access Act in their local communities.[22]

Shifting to state convention reactions to the issue of prayer in public schools, the District of Columbia Convention adopted a resolution in 1962 commending the Supreme Court "for restraining governmental agencies from undertaking the formulation of prayers for the American children and the American people."[23] "The Court did not outlaw prayer," stated the 1962 adopted report of the Christian Life Commission of the Baptist General Convention of Texas. Instead, "It made prayer free from political control."[24] The Baptist General Association of Virginia approved the 1962 report of its Religious Liberty Committee which interpreted the Court's decision to mean that "the state has many functions but one of them is not the composing of prayers for use in schools."[25]

State conventions have expressed similar sentiments up to the present. Virginia Baptists have been especially active in defending the Supreme Court decisions of 1962 and 1963, in supporting voluntary prayer in public schools, and in attacking proposed constitutional prayer amendments.[26] Baptists in other states, such as Texas and Louisiana,[27] have also addressed these subjects frequently.

Taking a position opposite that of the 1982 Southern Baptist Convention, several state conventions adopted strong statements in that year opposing the proposed prayer amendment of President Reagan. North Carolina was apparently the only state convention explicitly to endorse the proposed amendment,[28] although a resolution of the Kansas-Nebraska Convention seemed to imply support.[29]

Some of the conventions which opposed the proposed amendment called for a renewed protection of the "principles set out in the First Amendment including the right to practice voluntary prayer" (Alabama),[30] affirmed "the stand Baptists have taken in previous years" (Kentucky),[31] and acknowledged that the Supreme Court had not declared as "unconstitutional truly voluntary expressions of individual faith" (Louisiana).[32] Other states resolved that "we express our opposition to any effort of government to become involved in the writing of prayers or in the religious instruction of our children" (Missouri)[33] and urged United States Congressmen to vote against any amendment which "would endanger the freedom of religion guaranteed by the First Amendment" (Tennessee).[34] Texas Baptists reminded, "Baptists have strongly opposed legislatively-prescribed prayer in any form which amounts to state establishment of religion."[35] Baptists in Virginia claimed, "The United States Supreme Court has *never* forbidden voluntary prayer in the public schools of our country. It has ruled against government prescribed or prepared prayers and against schools that decide when and how voluntary prayer is to be offered."[36]

Selected News Media Reactions

Examination of selected *Baptist Press* releases and issues of Southern Baptist state newspapers for the two-year period from April 1982, to March 1984, clearly revealed the general thrust of Baptist attitudes toward one proposed prayer amendment, that of President Reagan.

Between March and June 1982, according to news reports, the Baptist Joint Committee on Public Affairs adopted a strongly worded statement opposing the proposed amendment and reaffirming its support for the 1962 and 1963 Supreme Court decisions banning state-mandated prayer and Bible reading in schools.[37] The executive director of the Baptist Joint Committee released a statement viewing it as objectionable "for the President to play petty politics with prayer. He knows that the Supreme Court has never banned prayer in schools. It can't. Real prayer is always free."[38] Several conservative Southern Baptist leaders were invited to a White House ceremony on May 6 to hear President Reagan's announcement that he planned to submit his proposed prayer amendment to Congress.[39] The editor of the Texas Baptist newspaper claimed that Reagan's proposed constitutional amendment could lead to government-written prayers and then admonished that "Baptists . . . must not contribute to the undoing of the First Amendment."[40] The editor of the New Mexico Baptist newspaper objected to passing Reagan's proposal because it "would put the government's hands in religion as it would provide for religious services [in public schools]."[41]

Between July and December 1982, *Baptist Press* reported that Edward E. McAteer, founder and president of Religious Roundtable, had both received White House backing to cultivate Southern Baptist support for President Reagan's proposed prayer amendment and had played a major role in shepherding a resolution favoring the proposed amendment through the Convention's Resolutions Committee in June by frequently advising committee chairman Norris W. Sydnor, Jr., a Religious Roundtable leader from Maryland.[42] At a breakfast sponsored by a religious liberty organization, the president of the Southern Baptist Radio and Television Commission commented, "No amount of semantic toedancing can change the fact that what the [Reagan] prayer amendment seeks is not voluntary prayer but forced religious rituals."[43] A staff member of the Baptist Joint Committee on Public Affairs described the proposed prayer amendment as "a false bill of goods" which was "nothing more than a return to the pre-1962 status quo, before the Supreme Court outlawed state-required and state-written public school devotionals."[44] Major editorials in the Missouri and Florida Baptist state newspapers opposed the adoption of the proposed prayer amendment.[45]

While the news media continued to note that some Southern Baptists favored passage of the proposed prayer amendment, most statements in 1983 and 1984 opposed its passage. Typical of the latter position was the claim of the editor of the North Carolina Baptist state newspaper, "Prayer must be voluntary, never forced. Ritual prayers are meaningless and to use a spiritual device to control a secular situation of misconduct and indifference in the classroom is to cheapen and degrade the true character of authentic prayer."[46]

In July 1983, President Reagan announced that he was sending to Congress a revised version of his proposed constitutional amendment on prayer in public schools to allay fears that his original proposed amendment would give federal and state governments the power to write prayers for schools. The general counsel of the Baptist Joint Committee responded to this revised proposal: "The fact that a constitutional amendment is unnecessary for truly voluntary prayer to exist in public schools is not altered by the addition of the words proposed by the White House staff. The new words contain legal loopholes which could lead to serious inroads into the principle of the separation of church and state."[47]

At the beginning of 1984, "equal access" bills were pending in both Houses of the United States Congress which would give secondary school students the same access to voluntary, student-initiated and student-controlled religious gatherings provided for other student-initiated nonacademic activities. Numerous Baptist leaders rallied behind this proposed legislation. The editor of the Kentucky Baptist state newspaper wrote: "Such equal access legislation is much needed. It would permit voluntary group religious exercises in public schools and it would greatly help school officials who understandably are confused as to what religious activities are permitted and what are not permitted by law in public schools."[48]

After the Senate rejected President Reagan's proposed

prayer amendment in March 1984, Southern Baptist Convention President James T. Draper, Jr., who had supported the proposed amendment, and Baptist Joint Committee on Public Affairs Executive Director James M. Dunn, who had opposed it, voiced common support for the equal access proposals being considered by Congress. Their unity symbolized the consolidation of many Southern Baptist leaders in favor of such legislation.

Selected Church-State Publication Reactions

Publications examined as sources for this section included the *Journal of Church and State,* published three times a year by the J. M. Dawson Institute of Church-State Studies of Baylor University, and *Report from the Capital,* published ten times a year by the Baptist Joint Committee on Public Affairs.

While the *Journal of Church and State* presented several major articles on prayer in public schools between 1962 and 1984, those by James E. Wood, Jr., editor of the journal (1959-1973, 1980-) and executive director of the Baptist Joint Committee (1972-1980), were especially helpful. He repeatedly defended the correctness of the 1962 and 1963 Supreme Court decisions on prayer and Bible reading in public schools and repeatedly denounced all proposals to amend the United States Constitution in order to provide state-sanctioned prayers to be used in these schools.[49]

For Wood the 1962 Supreme Court decision was "one of the most far-reaching and significant decisions relative to church and state to be made in America."[50] The issue at stake was that official prayers written by state authorities for use in public schools were unconstitutional since they represented a threat to religious liberty and the separation of church and state. Wood observed, "Prayer is a religious act and therefore cannot be sponsored by the state without violating the establishment clause of the First Amendment."[51]

Admitting that many people still do not know what the Supreme Court ruled in 1962 and 1963 regarding prayer and Bible reading in public schools, Wood noted that many efforts to rescind the Court's decisions through proposed constitutional amendments have ironically sought to restore "voluntary prayer" in these schools. "The premise is a false one since the Court never ruled against voluntary prayer in the public schools."[52] Strongly opposing all efforts to secure government-sponsored prayer in public schools because of its invasion of personal freedom, Wood concluded, "Legislating prayer in the public schools . . . is in harmony with neither authentic religion nor a free society."[53]

Report from the Capital included dozens of articles on prayer in public schools between 1962 and 1984. Through this publication, the staff of the Baptist Joint Committee on Public Affairs performed a significant service to Baptists by: (a) providing detailed news coverage and analyses of the Supreme Court decisions on prayer in public schools and of subsequent proposed prayer amendments; (b) citing the continuing support of the Baptist Joint Committee and of Baptist conventions, editors, and denominational leaders for the Supreme Court decisions and their opposition to proposed prayer amendments; (c) describing the constitutional and theological principles relating to prayer in public schools; and (d) offering constructive guidelines for dealing with the prayer issues at stake.

One quickly senses in the writings of Baptist Joint Committee staff members their personal, professional, and consistent commitment to the First Amendment of the United States Constitution and to the basic Baptist principles of religious liberty and the separation of church and state. They wrote with deep conviction, and they wrote convincingly. The following instructive samples of their writings attest that they were in touch with their Baptist heritage of freedom as they did their work on prayer issues.

C. Emanuel Carlson beautifully stated a common Baptist view in 1966 in commenting on a proposed constitutional amendment relating to prayer in public schools: "Among Baptists prayer is not a matter of social adjustment or of national heritage. It is understood to be communication between a person or people and God. Hence, attempts by public authorities to claim some permissive or regulatory control over prayer or worship causes apprehension among us."[54]

Opposing a different proposed prayer amendment, James M. Sapp in 1971 challenged government involvement in religion: "Government is not competent in the area of religion."[55] Because "prayers by school children or religious exercises in public schools is not an appropriate province of government . . . the government simply must not intrude in anyway into the personal religious lives of public school children."[56]

In responding to the mistaken notion of many that the Supreme Court in its 1962 and 1963 decisions had prohibited voluntary prayer from public schools, W. Barry Garrett wrote powerfully in 1971 that

> Rather than complaining about these decisions, every God-fearing person in the United States should praise the courts and the U. S. Constitution for holding the line and placing religious responsibility where it should be. Government religion, government sponsored religion, government establishment of religion, government endorsed religion is the antithesis to genuine New Testament principles.
>
> No government official be he a king, a president, a member of Congress, a member of the school board or a school teacher has a right to tell a school child when to pray, how to pray, or what to pray. . . . This is a sacred privilege that should be retained for the home, the church, the citadel of the individual soul.[57]

The views of James E. Wood, Jr., were similar to those

which he shared in the *Journal of Church and State* (discussed earlier).

James M. Dunn strongly repudiated President Reagan's 1982 announced intention to submit to Congress a proposed constitutional amendment on prayer.[58] Reagan's proposed amendment, he wrote, is "unneeded, unwanted, and unworkable."[59]

Also in 1982, John W. Baker described false premises behind Reagan's proposed prayer amendment, cited potential dangers to religious liberty posed by the possible adoption of the proposed amendment, and then concluded: "An amendment to 'put God back in the schools' is unnecessary and dangerous. Religious people should join their denominations in a vocal all-out campaign against the proposal."[60]

In 1983 Stan Hastey evaluated the original and revised versions of Reagan's proposed prayer amendment, claimed that neither version "answers the basic question of who will write the prayers school children will be expected to recite as part of their daily routine," posited that the proposal "deserves to fail," and predicted accurately that "the people's representatives in Congress are not going to accept a prayer amendment."[61]

Conclusion

Prayer and freedom go hand in hand in Baptist life. The biblical guarantee of direct access to God encourages Baptists to pray. Prayer, in turn, leads to increased freedom. In the early stages of their history, Baptists prayed passionately for freedom to practice their faith after the model of New Testament Christianity. A prayerful search for and healthy attachment to religious liberty became a goal that is still a vital part of the Baptist spirit.

The Bible reveals at least three important relationships between prayer and freedom. In the first, biblical persons prayed for freedom from limitations upon their own lives and/or the lives of others. Such limitations included physical illness, death, barrenness, sin, bondage, and distress. In the second, the people of Scripture prayed for personal freedom and strength to do God's will. The prayer life of Jesus is the supreme model for this relationship. In the third, persecution of the people of God led to some of the highest expressions of freedom in prayer. A lions' den, imprisonments, stonings, and the cross encouraged surges of prayer and liberty.

Early Baptists in England and America prayed with intensity in the face of considerable opposition from political and religious forces. Advocates of the biblical principles of religious liberty and the separation of church and state, Baptists marched into the future on the feet of prayer for freedom. Evidence is rampant that Baptists in many parts of the world continue to suffer infringements upon the practice of their faith. Baptist individuals, churches, associations, conventions, unions, federations, and the Baptist World Alliance persist in praying for the release of the captives. The liberating relevance of prayer in the life of Martin Luther King, Jr., illustrated effectively the essential relationship between prayer and freedom in the Baptist story.

Prayer and freedom in public schools has been a major issue in Baptist life, at least since 1962 when the Supreme Court prohibited the use of officially prescribed state-written prayers in these schools. Some Baptists have misunderstood the Supreme Court's intent and the implications of government-sponsored prayer, but most Baptists have opposed proposed constitutional amendments on school prayer. These proposed amendments, while allegedly providing for the restoration of voluntary prayer in public schools (which the Supreme Court did not and could not rule against), have actually provided for the reinstitution of government involvement in the prayer life of students in the schools (a practice which runs counter to the best wisdom of the Baptist heritage).

Generally, Baptist conventions, news media, and church-state publications have supported the Supreme Court's 1962 and 1963 decisions on prayer and Bible reading in public schools, have opposed proposed constitutional amendments designed to reverse these decisions, and have backed the equal access measure which became law in 1984.

The Baptist Joint Committee on Public Affairs has been a guiding light in educating Baptists to a fuller understanding of their responsibility in school prayer issues. The unyielding commitment of the agency to the First Amendment of the United States Constitution and to the Baptist heritage of freedom has made it a bulwark of strength to Baptists and to the entire nation every time that potential government intrusion into the prayer life of students in public schools has mounted. More prayer amendments will likely be proposed in the future, and the Baptist Joint Committee will continue to oppose them.

5

Lessons from Prayer History

Selected lessons from the prayer story of Baptists deserve attention since they can help in understanding some of the key thrusts and contributions of the Baptist heritage of prayer. The reduction of a large amount of historical research into a few basic lessons can also demonstrate further the practicality of this study. The lessons can highlight certain aspects of the prayer pilgrimage of Baptists that merit consideration by individuals, families, churches, and larger bodies as they assess the current status of prayer in their lives and make prayer plans for the future.

Lesson 1

Baptists view the Bible as the ultimate written authority on prayer. In their search for roots, Baptists look to the Bible for their primary teachings about prayer, and they turn to Jesus Christ for their supreme model in prayer. Baptist writings on prayer typically devote considerable space to passages of Scripture which state essential affirmations about prayer. Prayer accounts of such biblical persons as Hannah, David, Daniel, Jesus, Stephen, and Paul figure prominently in Baptist preaching and teaching.

Many writers refer to the failure of numerous Baptists to pray regularly and effectively, and they also discuss misuses of prayer. This suggests that Baptists need to give even more attention to biblical views and practices of prayer than they are accustomed to doing. Many passages in the Bible contain prayers and guidelines for praying. Christians are virtually without excuse in failing to pray and in mismanaging their relationship with God through prayer. The Bible clearly presents illustrations and actual occurrences of the need to pray constantly (1 Thess. 5:17), to pray intensely (Jas. 5:17), to pray boldly (Dan. 6:7-10), to pray expectantly (Matt. 7:7), to pray with faith (Matt. 21:22), and to pray in the Spirit (Eph. 6:18).

Careful study of prayer in the Bible is a fundamental requirement for the devotional life of Baptists. The quality and depth of prayer depend heavily upon reading and comprehending the nature, purpose, and types of prayer in biblical literature. Secondary sources are valuable for instruction in prayer, but no source can compete in value and authority with the primary source. Growth in prayer demands that Christians stay close to the textbook of their faith.

Lesson 2

Prayer is crucial to Baptist history, theology, and practice. Vital records of the Baptist heritage, such as church, associational, and convention minutes, amply demonstrate that Baptists have made prayer a priority as their story has emerged. Baptist biography supports the assertion that those individuals who have made the most constructive contributions to God and the church have been persons committed to prayer. The driving force behind the significant achievements of Baptists in missions, evangelism, stewardship, theological education, and other major enterprises has been their historic dedication to God in prayer.

Theology and devotion go hand in hand in Baptists' self-understanding. Baptist theology would be empty without prayer. What value would there be in having a resurrected Lord without a means of access to Him? Ponder the implications, if there were no prayer, for such Baptist doctrines as the priesthood of the believer, believer's baptism, regenerate church membership, and religious liberty. Prayer undergirds Baptist theology as a foundation supports a building. Further, prayer integrates the teachings of Baptists into a theology that attempts to reflect Scripture and magnify Jesus Christ.

Baptists engage in a wide range of important practices in living out their faith. They constitute new churches, they ordain new ministers, they observe the ordinances, they teach the Bible, they sing great hymns, they conduct business meetings, they participate in missions, and they perform other vital tasks. Prayer, another practice, is important in that it has a direct relationship with all the other practices. It adds meaning to them, it escalates their significance, and it invokes divine blessing upon them.

Lesson 3

Prayer is essential to the spiritual health of individuals, families, churches, and other Baptist bodies. In imitation of the prayer life of Jesus, Baptists have emphasized the urgency of private prayer by every Christian. Ironically, however, personal prayer on a daily basis is perhaps one of the most neglected disciplines of Baptists. Considering its potential values and the forces working against it in the hectic life-styles of many people today, the thrust of Baptist heritage in behalf of personal prayer continues to deserve constant visibility and promotion.

The records of Baptist history plainly show and boldly affirm the need for family prayer. The dangers to spiritual health in families are almost unlimited—lack of communication, marital breakdown, alcoholism, working patterns, and others. Besides preventing fracture, prayer can also nurture unity in family life. Prayer can also lead to healing in families where fracture has already occurred.

When individuals pray and when families pray, corporate

prayer in the church and in other Baptist bodies assumes an integrity that it may otherwise lack. Effective public prayer hinges on the quality of prayer that precedes it in private and family life. Baptists have always viewed prayer as a primary ingredient of public worship, and this is a standard which always needs to be maintained. A church which cherishes prayer is a church which loves God. Many public worship leaders may profit by heeding the encouragement of those Baptist writers who advocate increased preparation for public prayer.

Lesson 4

Prayer links Baptists together with all Christians in a common relationship with God. Through the years many Baptist groups have opposed participation in interdenominational organizations because of Baptist doctrine and polity. But prayer is a great common denominator which unites all Christendom. Baptists can join Methodists in praying for revival, they can join Lutherans in praying for forgiveness, they can join Pentecostals in praying for sensitivity to the Holy Spirit, and they can join one another in praying for peace around the world. Prayer moves Christians beyond denominational distinctives into a unifying experience of the faith.

Baptists even owe a large debt to other Christian traditions at the point of prayer. The earliest English Baptists emerged out of English Separatism. London Baptists of the 1670s relied heavily upon a Presbyterian doctrinal statement in developing their own confession of faith. Many Separate Baptists in America in the 1700s grew directly out of Congregationalism. The prayer patterns of these and other non-Baptist groups inevitably influenced those of Baptists.

Within Baptist ranks, prayer unites Baptists from all around the world into a common bond of devotion and purpose. The Baptist World Alliance facilitates such unity through its special days of prayer for men, women, and youth. The European Baptist Federation urges togetherness in prayer among the Baptists on a particular continent. The Baptist Federation of Canada sponsors joint prayer efforts among the Baptists of a specific country. These are only a few examples of united approaches in prayer which place Baptists of all nationalities closer to one another and closer to the will of God.

Lesson 5

The testimonies of the Baptist heritage show that the values of prayer are unlimited. Individuals point to changed lives, families point to growth in love, churches point to forward steps in stewardship, and denominations point to achievements in missions. The by-products of prayer are beyond estimation.

Perhaps Baptist leaders need to take more initiative in calling people to prayer. Who could possibly have predicted the spectacular results that would come from the 1784 prayer call of the Northampton Baptist Association in England? In addition to giving tremendous impetus to missions and revivalism, this one prayer call stimulated regularity in prayer meetings in many parts of the known Baptist world. No one knows what the Holy Spirit can accomplish through Christians totally committed to God in prayer.

Baptist writers have often cautioned against praying simply to enhance personal advantage. Because of the seriousness of such cautions, perhaps the observations of one more Baptist scholar may be helpful. Wayne E. Oates, renowned pastoral psychologist, wrote the following while considering the role of prayer in pastoral counseling:

> Prayer is a relationship. It is not a tool or a resource or any such means to some other end, however worthy that end may be. Communion with God, more so than any other relationship, has many dramatic and awe-inspiring side effects, such as healing, relaxation, and peace of mind. But

these are not the purpose of prayer. Communion with God is the love of God for his own sake alone.[1]

Lesson 6

Special prayer emphases help focus the attention of Baptists upon the relationship between prayer and specific dimensions of life. Baptists have used many ways to commit to God and ask His blessings upon efforts they have viewed as vital to the living out of their faith. These efforts have shown the desire of Baptists to keep their ministries within God's will. Through a variety of approaches, Baptists have creatively sought to communicate prayer as an exciting spiritual discipline.

Prayer deserves bold promotion. Baptists have encouraged prayer through many means; some of these are publications, days of prayer, prayer retreats, and prayer support teams. The purpose of these promotions has been to help believers to implement prayer as fully as possible. Special prayer efforts have benefitted missions, evangelism, and theological education. Prayer can be promoted in numerous channels and forms; it then gains a prominence in the Christian life of Baptists which it must have.

A couple of precautions concerning the use of special prayer emphases may be helpful. First, Baptist leaders may want to guard against developing and promoting too many emphases; such could weaken the attention given to each and make laypeople weary of them. Second, promotional schemes must never take priority over the significance of prayer as relationship with God. With precautions in mind, Baptists will still do well to remain close to their heritage as they continue to call one another to special prayer to meet extraordinary challenges.

Lesson 7

Prayer in behalf of missions has been and must continue to be paramount in Baptist life. Baptist commitment to the Great Commission of Jesus means first, and perhaps foremost, that prayer should precede, accompany, and support the sending of missionaries, money, and supplies to mission points around the globe. Prayer for missions is healthy in that it thrusts the focal point of the one who prays outside of self, it is necessary in that it undergirds the missionary mandate of the New Testament, and it is satisfying in that it gives everyone who prays an opportunity to engage in the mission task.

The letters of the apostle Paul, missionary par excellence, vividly portray the importance which he assigned to prayer for missions. Baptists caught the spirit of Paul's prayer vision when William Carey, Luther Rice, and other mission pioneers began to help them see the need to support missions. The famous English Baptist prayer call of 1784 and a whole host of special prayer emphases since then have deeply sensitized most Baptists to the duty and privilege to pray for missions.

Missions needs to remain a priority item on the prayer agenda of Baptists. Acceptance of this challenge will keep them close to the call of God to share the gospel with all people. The Baptist heritage of a strong mission consciousness and of well-functioning mission support agencies merits careful evaluation and meaningful perpetuation. Aided by the prayers of the faithful, Baptists will continue their ministry of sharing Jesus, the Light of the world.

Lesson 8

The family-oriented, churchwide, weekly prayer meeting seems to be in trouble in many Baptist churches. One factor is the competition of other midweek meetings. Another is the multiplication of other kinds of prayer meetings by various groups in churches. Still another is the low priority given to churchwide prayer meetings as reflected in inadequate preparation, lack of creative approaches, and low attendance. The significance of prayer meetings to many Baptists of the past suggests, by contrast, that current patterns are failing to meet the prayer needs of many congregations.

Baptists need to counter such negative trends with positive action. A church which renews the family-oriented, churchwide, weekly prayer meeting can more effectively live out its New Testament role as the "family of God" and can establish a stronger basis for expecting its families to pray together at home. Such renewal can also bring families together for prayer in the setting of the church as a healthy preventive to the all-too-common breakdown of marriages and families. Besides family needs, many other considerations in Baptist life regularly deserve the full attention of the whole congregation meeting together for prayer.

What about the apparent obstacles to such prayer meetings? A church can eliminate the element of competition created by other midweek meetings simply by rearranging its schedule and making the prayer meeting the church's top midweek priority. Vigorously encourage the attendance of the entire congregation at the prayer meeting. If deemed helpful, consider taking official church action to discourage any other activities during this time slot. The prayer meeting can then become the focal point for the midweek gathering of the church from which family members can then disperse to other meetings.

Since time is an important factor, consider condensing the prayer meeting to a maximum of thirty minutes. Plan each prayer meeting weeks in advance. Prepare thoroughly for each event. Use a variety of leaders (ordained and lay). Use innovative and stimulating approaches. Keep the meetings simple, and make them appealing to children, youth, and adults. Urge family members to sit together, and highlight the role of families in the meetings.

Lesson 9

A prayer meeting will serve its name and purpose best if devoted primarily to prayer. Few Baptists underestimate the importance of Bible study and preaching. The Baptist stress on Sunday School and regular Sunday worship services shows this to be true. But to use the weekly midweek prayer meeting mainly to conduct a churchwide Bible study class or to preach another sermon inevitably neglects the primary function of prayer meetings—to pray.

Consider converting at least two-thirds of every prayer meeting into a worship experience of determining prayer requests, actually praying, and using various prayer-related resources. After securing prayer requests from all who wish to share them (including children and youth), the prayer meeting leader can then direct the prayer time in a creative way. Make provision each week for children, youth, and adults to verbalize some of the prayers. Particularly in the case of children and youth, the prayer meeting leader may want to talk with them several days in advance, both to invite them to pray aloud in the prayer meeting and to assign them special points of concern so that they might prepare to pray. In this manner, encouragement in prayer can helpfully precede the praying.

In coordinating the prayer time, the leader can use appropriate hymns, Bible readings, sentence prayers, silent prayer, prayer lists, responsive readings, written prayers from the past, prayer thoughts from classics of Christian devotion, and other approaches and resources. Each prayer leader is urged to be as innovative as possible so that prayer meeting will be a place where all ages will want to go.

Consider using the remaining one-third of each prayer meeting as a time of instruction in prayer. This instruction can focus upon such topics as the following.

- The place of prayer in the Bible

- The teachings of Jesus regarding prayer
- The role of prayer in church history
- The significance of prayer in Christian theology
- The nature, meaning, and purpose of prayer
- The importance of preparation for prayer
- Helps for personal, family, and public prayer
- The values of prayer

The pastor and perhaps other church staff members plus a church-elected Prayer Meeting Committee should be responsible for planning and promoting prayer meetings, enlisting and training prayer meeting leaders, providing leaders with appropriate resources, and evaluating the meetings.

Lesson 10

Prayer and freedom go hand in hand in Baptist life. Baptists extract freedom from biblical teachings about prayer, insert freedom into their understanding of the nature of prayer, and expect freedom in their attitudes toward prayer in public schools. Viewing prayer as the ultimate expression of human freedom and freedom as the ultimate result of prayer, Baptists relate the two realities in deliberate fashion.

Baptists reject ecclesiastical and governmental intrusion into anyone's prayer life. They collided with the efforts of the Church of England in Colonial America to suppress their freedom of worship, and they have collided with several unsuccessful efforts of various national leaders in recent years to secure government-sponsored prayer in public schools. Protection of free prayer lies at the root of the traditional Baptist defense of religious liberty and the separation of church and state.

Perhaps Baptists' greatest weakness in freedom in prayer is their failure to use this freedom more fully. The demands of life sometimes cause individuals and families to go for extended periods of time without praying at all. The result of such inattention to prayer can only be a loss of freedom. As Christians move away from their relationship with God in prayer, they obligate themselves, either consciously or subconsciously, to influences which work against their freedom in Christ. A helpful word in this regard may be the call of the freedom-loving apostle Paul for all Christians to pray constantly (Rom. 12:12).

Conclusion

The prayer story of Baptists is a magnificent account of the efforts of a specific group of God's people to communicate with Him. The story has been in the making for almost four centuries. During these years, Baptists have found prayer to be the root of all spiritual disciplines. Through prayer they have received power and strength from God to help build a denomination committed to sharing the good news to all people. Lessons have emerged from prayer developments in Baptist life. These lessons, at the least, offer opportunities for discussion. At the most, they present a challenge for contemporary Baptists to surge forward in their piety to levels of devotion and relationship with God never before attained.

Notes

CHAPTER 1

1. Walter H. Burgess, *John Smith the Se-Baptist, Thomas Helwys, and the First Baptist Church in England* (London: James Clarke and Co., 1911), pp. 170-71.

2. William Rutherford, *Church Members' Guide for Baptist Churches,* second edition (Atlanta: James P. Harrison & Co., 1887), p. 108.

3. George W. Truett, *Follow Thou Me* (Nashville: Sunday School Board, SBC, 1924), pp. 13-15.

4. E. Y. Mullins, *Christianity at the Cross Roads* (Nashville: Sunday School Board, SBC, 1924), p. 93.

5. William Owen Carver, *Thou When Thou Prayest* (Nashville: Sunday School Board, SBC, 1928), p. 3.

6. W. T. Conner, *The Faith of the New Testament* (Nashville: Broadman Press, 1940), pp. 143-44.

7. Fred L. Fisher, *Prayer in the New Testament* (Philadelphia: Westminster Press, 1964), p. 9.

8. James Leo Garrett, Jr., "A Theology of Prayer," *Southwestern Journal of Theology,* 14:7, Spring 1972.

9. Herbert C. Jackson and Lynn E. May, Jr., "Carey, William," *Encyclopedia of Southern Baptists* (Nashville: Broadman Press, 1958), 1, p. 231.

10. R. Keith Parks, statement to Executive Committee, SBC, 20 September 1982.

11. E. Y. Mullins, *The Christian Religion in Its Doctrinal Expression* (Nashville: Sunday School Board, SBC, 1917), p. 274.

12. E. Y. Mullins, *The Axioms of Religion* (Philadelphia: American Baptist Publication Society, 1908), pp. 70, 73.

13. Francis Wayland, "Circular Letter," *Minutes,* Shaftsbury Association (Vermont), 1813, p. 13.
14. Fisher Humphreys, *The Heart of Prayer* (Nashville: Broadman Press, 1980), p. 47.
15. J. P. Allen, "Prayer—Perspective from the Pulpit," *Southwestern Journal of Theology,* 14:69, Spring 1972.
16. William Roy McNutt, *Worship in the Churches* (Philadelphia: Judson Press, 1941), p. 84.
17. A. T. Robertson, *Practical and Social Aspects of Christianity: The Wisdom of James* (New York: George H. Doran Co., 1915), p. 258.
18. H. E. Fosdick, *The Meaning of Prayer* (London: Collins Press, 1915; 4th Fontana Books impression, 1968), pp. 85, 196.
19. W. T. Conner, *A System of Christian Doctrine* (Nashville: Sunday School Board, SBC, 1924), p. 488.
20. Conner, *The Faith of the New Testament,* p. 150.
21. Ernest A. Payne, "Public Prayer," *The Baptist Quarterly,* New Series, 2:129-30, July 1924.
22. A. D. Gillette, ed., *Minutes of the Philadelphia Baptist Association from A.D. 1707 to A.D. 1807* (Philadelphia: American Baptist Publication Society, 1851), p. 398.
23. E. Glenn Hinson, *The Reaffirmation of Prayer* (Nashville: Broadman Press, 1979), p. 15.
24. Robertson, p. 264.
25. Conner, *The Faith of the New Testament,* pp. 150-51.
26. W. T. Conner, *Gospel Doctrines* (Nashville: Sunday School Board, SBC, 1925), p. 107.
27. J. M. Pendleton, *Christian Doctrines: A Compendium of Theology* (Philadelphia: American Baptist Publication Society, 1878), p. 309.
28. *Annual,* Southern Baptist Convention, 1881, p. 28.
29. Stephen Wright, comp., *History of the Shaftsbury Baptist Association from 1781 to 1853* (Troy, N. Y.: A. G. Johnson, 1853), p. 113.
30. McNutt, p. 88.
31. William L. Lumpkin, *Baptist Confessions of Faith,* revised edition (Valley Forge: Judson Press, 1969), p. 281; *A Confession of Faith . . . Adopted by the Baptist Association Met at Philadelphia, September 25, 1742* (Philadelphia: Anderson and Meehan, 1818), p. 55.

32. P. H. Mell, *The Doctrine of Prayer; Its Utility; and Its Relation to Providence* (New York: Sheldon & Co., 1876), pp. 37-44.

33. Sermon by E. M. Levy in Joseph Belcher, *The Baptist Pulpit in the United States,* second edition (New York: Edward H. Fletcher, 1853), p. 257.

34. *Flashes of Thought; Being One Thousand Choice Extracts from the Works of C. H. Spurgeon* (London: Passmore & Alabaster, 1906), p. 328.

35. James Leo Garrett, Jr., "Prayer," *Encyclopedia of Southern Baptists* (Nashville: Broadman Press, 1958), 2, p. 1103.

36. Lumpkin, p. 329.

37. *Minutes of the General Conference of the Freewill Baptist Connection* (Dover: Freewill Baptist Printing Establishment, 1859), p. 55.

38. *Year Book,* American Baptist Convention, 1960, p. 66.

39. Andrew Gunton Fuller, ed., *The Complete Works of the Rev. Andrew Fuller* (Boston: Lincoln, Edmands & Co., 1833), 2, p. 97.

40. *Flashes of Thought,* p. 325.

41. Edward T. Hiscox, *The Baptist Church Directory* (New York: Sheldon & Co., 1859), p. 143.

42. Carver, p. 20.

43. Ibid., pp. 21-22.

44. Jack R. Taylor, *Prayer: Life's Limitless Reach* (Nashville: Broadman Press, 1977), p. 12.

45. Gillette, pp. 44, 59, 71, 72, 76-77, 79, 80, 87, 90, 92, 98, 110, 115, 121, 126, 266, 403.

46. *Minutes,* Stonington Association (Connecticut), 1774 (p. 16 of reprint in 1845 minutes).

47. Wright, p. 113.

48. Ibid., p. 198.

49. Ibid., pp. 231-34.

50. Ibid., p. 234.

51. Lemuel Burkitt and Jesse Read, *A Concise History of the Kehukee Baptist Association,* rev., Henry L. Burkitt (Philadelphia: Lippincott, Grambo and Co., 1850), p. 133.

52. Jesse Mercer, *A History of the Georgia Baptist Association* (Washington, Ga.: n.n., 1838), pp. 130, 152, 206, 340.

53. Olinthus Gregory and Joseph Belcher, eds., *The Works of the*

Rev. Robert Hall (New York: Harper & Brothers, 1854), 3, pp. 131, 133.

54. Irah Chase, "On Prayer" (Philadelphia: American Baptist Publication Society, n.d.), p. 5.

55. Duke K. McCall, "How to Maintain Family Worship" (Nashville: Sunday School Board, SBC, 1950), p. 8.

56. Ibid., pp. 4-8.

57. Claude L. Howe, Jr., "Family Worship in Baptist Life," *Baptist History and Heritage,* 17:53, January 1982.

58. Franklin M. Segler, *Christian Worship: Its Theology and Practice* (Nashville: Broadman Press, 1967), p. 109.

59. John A. Broadus, *A Treatise on the Preparation and Delivery of Sermons,* sixth edition (Philadelphia: Smith, English & Co., 1875), p. 492.

60. Gregory and Belcher, p. 135.

61. Broadus, p. 494.

62. Edward T. Hiscox, *The New Directory for Baptist Churches* (Philadelphia: American Baptist Publication Society, 1894), p. 225.

63. *Flashes of Thought,* p. 326.

64. McNutt, p. 99.

65. Ibid.

66. Ernest A. Payne, Stephen F. Winward, and James W. Cox, comps., *Ministers' Worship Manual* (New York: World Publishing Co., 1969), p. xv.

67. Francis Wayland, *Notes of the Principles and Practices of Baptist Churches* (New York: Sheldon, Blakeman & Co., 1858), p. 223.

68. Hiscox, *The Baptist Church Directory,* pp. 46-47.

69. Segler, p. 111.

70. Hinson, p. 12.

71. Ibid.

72. Ibid., pp. 16, 25.

73. Segler, pp. 118-20.

74. Carver, p. 17.

75. McNutt, p. 85.

CHAPTER 2

1. Ernest A. Payne, *The Fellowship of Believers: Baptist Thought and Practice Yesterday and Today,* revised edition (London: Carey Kingsgate Press, 1952), p. 108.

2. R. E. E. Harkness, "Origin of the Prayer-Meeting Among English and American Baptists," *The Chronicle,* 1:149, October 1938.

3. Payne, p. 108.

4. G. Thomas Halbrooks, "Prayer Meeting," *Encyclopedia of Southern Baptists,* (Nashville: Broadman Press, 1982), 4, p. 2,421.

5. Fred L. Fisher, *Prayer in the New Testament* (Philadelphia: Westminster Press, 1964), p. 185.

6. Halbrooks, p. 2,421.

7. Roger Hayden, ed., *The Records of a Church of Christ in Bristol, 1640-1687* (Gateshead: Printed for the Bristol Record Society, 1974), p. 114.

8. Ibid., p. 161.

9. Ibid., p. 202.

10. Ibid., p. 223.

11. Ibid., p. 252.

12. Harkness, pp. 150-154.

13. Hayden, p. 235.

14. Ibid., p. 244.

15. Ibid., p. 249.

16. Ibid., p. 255.

17. "Minutes from Olde Pennepack Record Books," *The Chronicle,* 1:126, July 1938.

18. Ibid., p. 127.

19. Harkness, p. 155.

20. W. T. Whitley, ed., *Minutes of the General Assembly of the General Baptist Churches in England* (London: Kingsgate Press, 1910), p. 142.

21. Harkness, p. 156.

22. Payne, p. 108.

23. Harkness, pp. 156, 159-160.

24. See A. D. Gillette, ed., *Minutes of the Philadelphia Association from A.D. 1707 to A.D. 1807* (Philadelphia: American Baptist Publication Society, 1851), pp. 28-343.

25. Ibid., p. 35.

26. Wood Furman, comp., *A History of the Charleston Association of Baptist Churches in the State of South Carolina* (Charleston: J. Hoff, 1811), p. 15.

27. Halbrooks, p. 2,421.

28. Ernest A. Payne, *The Prayer Call of 1784* (London: Baptist Laymen's Missionary Movement, 1941), p. 1. The description of the prayer call and its results is based on this source (pp. 1-12).

29. John Rippon, *The Baptist Annual Register for 1790, 1791, 1792, and Part of 1793* (London: Dilly, Button, and Thomas, n.d.), 1, p. 60.

30. Ibid., p. 105.

31. Ibid., p. 107.

32. Lemuel Burkitt and Jesse Read, *A Concise History of the Kehukee Baptist Association,* rev., Henry L. Burkitt (Philadelphia: Lippincott, Grambo and Co., 1850), p. 118.

33. Arthur B. Strickland, *The Great American Revival* (Cincinnati: Standard Press, 1934), p. 45.

34. Ibid.

35. Ibid., pp. 46-47.

36. *Minutes,* Warren Baptist Association (Rhode Island), 1795, p. 6.

37. *Minutes,* Leyden Baptist Association (Vermont), 1795, p. 6.

38. Stephen Wright, comp., *History of the Shaftsbury Baptist Association, from 1781 to 1853* (Troy, N.Y.: A. G. Johnson, 1853), p. 46.

39. Ibid.

40. Ibid., pp. 115-16.

41. Gillette, pp. 74-87, 132-55, 159-70.

42. Ibid., p. 306.

43. Ibid., pp. 326-438.

44. Jesse Mercer, *A History of the Georgia Baptist Association* (Washington, GA: n.n., 1838), p. 36.

45. Furman, pp. 25-26.

46. Basil Manly, *Mercy and Judgment: A Discourse Containing Some Fragments of the History of the Baptist Church in Charleston, S. C.* (n.p.: Knowles, Vose and Co., 1837), p. 58.

47. George W. Purefoy, *A History of the Sandy Creek Baptist Association from Its Organization in A.D. 1758, to A.D. 1858* (New York: Sheldon & Co., 1859), p. 107.

48. *Proceedings,* Triennial Convention, 1817, pp. 133-34.

49. Hosea Holcombe, *A History of the Rise and Progress of the Baptists in Alabama* (Philadelphia: King and Baird, 1840; reprinted in Bessemer, AL: West Jefferson County Historical Society, 1975), pp. 140-41.

50. *Minutes,* Hudson River Baptist Association (New York), 1829, p. 9; *Minutes,* Louisiana Baptist State Convention, 1860, p. 9.

51. Edward T. Hiscox, *The Baptist Church Directory* (New York: Sheldon & Co., 1859), p. 39.

52. Edward T. Hiscox, *The New Directory for Baptist Churches* (Philadelphia: American Baptist Publication Society, 1894), p. 236.

53. *Annual,* Southern Baptist Convention (hereafter SBC), 1881, p. 28.

54. *Annual,* SBC, 1883, pp. 26-27.

55. *Annual,* SBC, 1888, p. 15.

56. *Annual,* SBC, 1892, p. XLVII of Foreign Mission Board Report.

57. Halbrooks, p. 2,421.

58. Blanche Sydnor White, *First Baptist Church, Richmond, 1780-1955* (Richmond: Whittet & Shepperson, n.d.), pp. 25-26; Lynn E. May, Jr., *The First Baptist Church of Nashville, Tennessee, 1820-1970* (Nashville: First Baptist Church, 1970), pp. 41-42; Albert W. Wardin, Jr., *Baptists in Oregon* (Portland: Judson Baptist College, 1969), p. 25.

59. *Annual,* Georgia Baptist Convention, 1824, p. 4.

60. *Minutes of the General Conference of the Freewill Baptist Connection* (Dover: Freewill Baptist Printing Establishment, 1859), p. 46.

61. Mary Webb, "Address of the Female Society, in Boston, to the Female Friends of Zion," *The Massachusetts Baptist Missionary Magazine,* March 1812, p. 156.

62. Mary Webb, "An Address from 'the Boston Female Society, for Missionary Purposes,' to Females Professing Godliness," *The Massachusetts Baptist Missionary Magazine,* March 1813, pp. 281-82.

63. White, p. 27.

64. *The Declaration of Faith, Church Covenant, and Rules of Order of the First Baptist Church, Philadelphia* (Philadelphia: King & Baird, 1851), p. 22.

65. Hiscox, *The Baptist Church Directory,* p. 40.

66. Hiscox, *The New Directory for Baptist Churches,* pp. 235-36.

67. Hiscox, *The Baptist Church Directory,* p. 40.

68. *Minutes,* Roanoke Baptist Association (Virginia), 1859, p. 16.

69. Lee N. Allen, *The First 150 Years: Montgomery's First Baptist Church, 1829-1979* (Montgomery: First Baptist Church, 1979), p. 141.

70. Hiscox, *The New Directory for Baptist Churches,* p. 236.

71. Ibid., p. 238.

72. H. Harvey, *The Pastor: His Qualifications and Duties* (Philadelphia: American Baptist Publication Society, 1879), p. 56.

73. Hiscox, *The New Directory for Baptist Churches,* p. 232.

74. Payne, *The Fellowship of Believers,* pp. 108-09.

CHAPTER 3

1. William L. Lumpkin, *Baptist Confessions of Faith,* revised edition (Valley Forge: Judson Press, 1969), pp. 122, 187, 194, 212, 226, 287, 319-20.

2. Ibid., p. 287; *A Confession of Faith . . . Adopted by the Baptist Association Met at Philadelphia, September 25, 1742* (Philadelphia: Anderson and Meehan, 1818), p. 63.

3. Thomas Grantham, *Christianismus Primitivus; or the Ancient Christian Religion* (London: Printed for Francis Smith, 1678), pp. 144-47.

4. Adam Taylor, *The History of the English General Baptists,* I (London: T. Bore, 1818), p. 429.

5. Morgan Edwards, *The Customs of Primitive Churches* (n.p.: n.n., 1774), p. 96.

6. A. D. Gillette, ed., *Minutes of the Philadelphia Baptist Association from A.D. 1707, to A.D. 1807* (Philadelphia: American Baptist Publication Society, 1851), pp. 167-68.

7. William G. McLoughlin, ed., *The Diary of Isaac Backus,* I (Providence, R.I.: Brown University Press, 1979), p. 28.

8. See, for example, ibid., pp. 94-95, 496.

9. Joseph B. Cook, *The Nature of a Fast. A Sermon Delivered . . . November 14, 1811* (Charleston, SC: Printed for the Presbyterian Society, 1813), pp. 6-7.

10. Ibid., pp. 7-13.

11. Edward Bean Underhill, ed., *Records of the Churches of Christ Gathered at Fenstanton, Warboys and Hexham, 1644-1720* (London: Haddon, Brothers, and Co., 1854), pp. 72, 187-90, 243.

12. Ibid., p. 244.

13. Ibid., p. 247.

14. Roger Hayden, ed., *The Records of a Church of Christ in Bristol, 1640-1687* (Gateshead: Printed for the Bristol Record Society, 1974), pp. 114-244.

15. W. T. Whitley, ed., *The Church Books of Ford or Cuddington and Amersham in the County of Bucks* (London: Printed for the Baptist Historical Society by Kingsgate Press, 1912), pp. 203-23.

16. Ibid., pp. 50-120.

17. "Minutes from Olde Pennepack Record Books," *The Chronicle,* 1:126, July 1938.

18. Robert I. Devin, *A History of the Grassy Creek Baptist Church* (Raleigh: Edwards, Broughton & Co., 1880), p. 88.

19. Leah Townsend, *South Carolina Baptists, 1670-1805* (Florence, S.C.: Florence Printing Co., 1935), p. 93.

20. W. T. Hundley, *History of Mattaponi Baptist Church, King and Queen County, Virginia* (Richmond: Appeals Press, n.d.), p. 472.

21. Gillette, pp. 28, 33, 71, 170, 292, 306.

22. Reuben Aldridge Guild, *Chaplain Smith and the Baptists or Life, Journals, Letters, and Addresses of the Rev. Hezekiah Smith of Haverhill, Massachusetts, 1737-1805* (Philadelphia: American Baptist Publication Society, 1885), p. 157.

23. *Annual,* Southern Baptist Convention (hereafter SBC), 1867, p. 2.

24. Bobbie Sorrill, "The History of the Week of Prayer for Foreign Missions," *Baptist History and Heritage,* 5:29-30, October, 1980; Bobbie Sorrill, "Week of Prayer for Home Missions and Annie Armstrong Easter Offering," *Encyclopedia of Southern Baptists* (Nashville: Broadman Press, 1982), 4, p. 2541.

25. Garnett Ryland, *The Baptists of Virginia, 1699-1926* (Richmond: Virginia Board of Missions and Education, 1955), p. 337.

26. *Annual,* SBC, 1977, p. 27.

27. Johnnie B. McCracken, "Homebounds Enroll in Prayer Ministry," *Baptist Press,* 10 July 1981, p. 1.

28. "Missions Prayer Plan," insert in *The Baptist Program,* May 1982, p. 2.

29. Roy Jennings, "Brotherhood Commission, SBC," *Encyclopedia of Southern Baptists* (Nashville, Broadman Press, 1982), 4, p. 2,132.

30. Anita Bowden, "Emeritus Missionary Takes Prayer Responsibility," *Baptist Press,* 16 February 1981, p. 6.

31. "HMB Appoints 33 Missionaries; Names Prayer Line Director," *Biblical Recorder,* 1 October 1983, p. 5.

32. "The CBOMB Prayer Line," *The Enterprise,* Winter, 1982-1983, cover page 4.

33. *Annual,* SBC, 1962, p. 66.

34. *Annual,* Northern Baptist Convention (hereafter NBC), 1908, p. 85.

35. *Annual,* NBC, 1922, pp. 100-101.

36. *Annual,* NBC, 1925, p. 587.

37. *Annual,* NBC, 1933, pp. 68-69.

38. Registration form distributed by 1984 Baptist Prayer Conference.

39. C. E. Autrey, *Basic Evangelism* (Grand Rapids: Zondervan Publishing House, 1959), pp. 86, 114-116, 122.

40. *Annual,* SBC, 1937, p. 89.

41. *Year Book,* American Baptist Convention (hereafter ABC), 1955, p. 113; 1956, p. 83.

42. *Annual,* SBC, 1970, p. 71.

43. "Prayer Requested for Europe Crusade," *European Baptist Press Service* (hereafter *EBPS*), 5 August 1963, p. 1.

44. "French Baptists Hold Prayer Meetings for Campaign," *EBPS,* 17 December 1966, p. 3.

45. "How Men Can Help in the Crusade," *The Baptist World,* 14:12, November 1967; "January 14 Named Day of Prayer," *The Baptist World,* 14:3, December 1967.

46. Doris DeVault, "PACT," *Encyclopedia of Southern Baptists* (Nashville: Broadman, 1982), 4, p. 2404.

47. Ibid.; Betty Brown, "Woman's Missionary Union," *Encyclopedia of Southern Baptists,* (Nashville: Broadman Press, 1971), 3, p. 2,056.

48. "Program Memorandum" (Number 49 00 00) of the Evangelism Section, Home Mission Board, 1982.

49. Program brochures of Evangelism Section, Home Mission Board, relating to each National Conference on Prayer for Spiritual Awakening, 1981 and 1982.

50. Program brochure of Evangelism Section, Home Mission Board, relating to the "Prayer for Spiritual Awakening Seminar," 1982.

51. Jim Newton, "Evangelism Directors Plan for Simultaneous Revivals," *Baptist Press,* 7 December 1983, p. 2.

52. Mrs. Edgar Bates, "The Baptist Women's Day of Prayer," *Official Report,* Baptist World Congress, 1965, p. 368; Barbara Yeager, "Baptist Women's World Day of Prayer," *Encyclopedia of Southern Baptists* (Nashville: Broadman Press, 1982), 4, p. 2109.

53. "Baptists Expect a Million for Women's World Day of Prayer," *EBPS,* October 12, 1979, p. 2.

54. Mrs. Edgar Bates, "The Value of Corporate Prayer," *The Baptist World,* 11:15, September 1965.

55. "Baptist Men's Worldwide Day of Witness and Prayer," *The Baptist World,* 23:4-5, January 1976; 24:9, February, 1977; 29:4, March 1982.

56. "Baptist Youth Day of Prayer," *EBPS,* 30 May 1983, p. 1.

57. *Official Report,* Baptist World Congress, 1950, p. 341; "Resolution," *The Baptist World,* 3:1, December 1956; "Baptists Called to Prayer for World Peace," *The Baptist World,* 19:1, April 1972; "Baptists Called to Prayer for Peace," *EBPS,* 7 December 1973, p. 1; "October 23: Day of Prayer for Peace," *The Baptist World,* 32:8, September 1977.

58. *Year Book,* NBC, 1942, pp. 259-260.

59. *Annual,* SBC, 1944, p. 150.

60. *Year Book,* NBC, 1948, p. 131.

61. *Year Book,* ABC, 1956, p. 91; 1957, pp. 99-100.

62. "Baptists in Japan Pray for Vietnam Peace," *EBPS,* 14 December 1967, p. 3; "Swedish Baptists Asked to Pray for Indochina," *EBPS,* 29 June 1972, p. 3.

63. E. Glenn Hinson, "Hopeful Happenings for Peace," *Baptist Peacemaker,* 2:1, January 1982; "Louisville Group Plans Prayers for

World Peace," *Florida Baptist Witness*, 27 May 1982, p. 4; "Strategies for Peacemaking," promotional brochure for A National Peace Convocation, Louisville, Kentucky, 5-7 August 1982.

64. "Planning Guide: Day of Prayer for World Peace," produced by Christian Life Commission, SBC, 1984, pp. 2-11.

65. Walter Rauschenbusch, *Prayers of the Social Awakening* (Boston: Pilgrim Press, 1910), p. 12.

66. "Negro Baptists Call for Day of Prayer," *The Baptist World*, 3:6, April 1956.

67. *Annual*, Baptist General Convention of Texas, 1964, p. 31.

68. "Irish Leaders Issue Prayer Call," *EBPS*, 21 November 1969, p. 3.

69. *Proceedings*, Triennial Convention, 1814, p. 7; 1817, p. 133.

70. *Annual*, SBC, 1880, p. 33.

71. *Annual*, NBC, 1932, pp. 120, 146, 206; 1933, p. 278; 1934, pp. 47, 48, 50, 53.

72. "Prayer Effort for L. A. Convention Coming Along," *Biblical Recorder*, 14 March 1981, p. 6.

73. Trent C. Butler, "Seminaries Observe Day of Prayer," *EBPS*, 5 November 1975, p. 4.

74. Stephen P. Carleton, "California Baptist College," *Encyclopedia of Southern Baptists* (Nashville: Broadman Press, 1982), 4, p. 2,141.

75. Bill J. Leonard, "Southern Baptist Theological Seminary, Endowed Chairs of," *Encyclopedia of Southern Baptists* (Nashville: Broadman Press, 1982), 4, p. 2,478.

76. Art Toalston, "Southwestern Plans 'Chair of Prayer,'" *Baptist Press*, 3 May 1984, pp. 4-5.

77. "Prayer Calendar," published by the Canadian Baptist Federation, October-December, 1984, p. 1.

78. *Annual*, SBC, 1960, p. 75.

79. Ernest D. Standerfer and Michael L. Speer, "Giving Trends in the 1970s," *Encyclopedia of Southern Baptists* (Nashville: Broadman Press, 1982), 4 p. 2,250.

80. *Annual*, SBC, 1980, p. 37.

81. Douglas L. Anderson, secretary, Family Ministry Depart-

ment, Sunday School Board, SBC, personal letter, 28 September 1983, p. 2.

82. Richard L. Shepherd, personal letter, June 24, 1982, pp. 1-4, plus attachments; "Prayer Support Ministries of the Cottage Hill Baptist Church," promotional leaflet, p. 3.

83. *Flashes of Thought; Being One Thousand Choice Extracts from the Works of C. H. Spurgeon* (London: Passmore & Alabaster, 1906), p. 327.

CHAPTER 4

1. Robert A. Baker, *A Baptist Source Book: With Particular Reference to Southern Baptists* (Nashville: Broadman Press, 1966), pp. 33-34.

2. *Minutes,* Warren Baptist Association (Rhode Island), 1774, pp. 7-8.

3. "World-Wide Day of Prayer, March 15, to Petition Restoration of Liberty to Spanish Evangelicals," *The Baptist World,* 6:1, March 1959.

4. "Day of Prayer in Congo Churches for Angolan Refugees," *European Baptist Press Service* (hereafter *EBPS*), 30 October 1962, p. 1.

5. "Imprisoned Missionaries Conduct Daily Prayer Services in Jail," *EBPS,* 28 September 1965, p. 2.

6. "French Baptists Issue Call to Prayer for Burundi," *EBPS,* 16 June 1972, p. 1.

7. Harold A. Carter, *The Prayer Tradition of Black People* (Valley Forge: Judson Press, 1976), p. 106.

8. Carol B. Franklin, "Georgi Vins Worships with Carter; Future Plans Uncertain," *Report from the Capital,* 34:4, 12 May 1979.

9. *Annual,* Southern Baptist Convention (hereafter SBC), 1971, p. 78.

10. *Annual,* SBC, 1974, p. 77.

11. *Annual,* SBC, 1975, p. 73.

12. James E. Wood, Jr., "Legislating Prayer in the Public Schools," *Journal of Church and State,* 23:208, Spring 1981.

13. Stan Hastey, "School Prayer: Reviewing 22 Years of Turbulence," *Baptist Press,* 28 March 1984, p. 2.

14. Baptist Joint Committee on Public Affairs, "Equal Access Fact Sheet," undated, p. 1.

15. Larry Chesser, "Equal Access Act Is Milestone in Religion-in-Schools Debate," *Baptist Press,* 3 August 1984, p. 1.

16. Stan Hastey, "School Prayer: Where We Are and How We Got There," *Baptist Courier,* 29 March 1984, p. 9.

17. *Annual,* SBC, 1963, p. 259.

18. *Annual,* SBC, 1972, p. 248.

19. *Annual,* SBC, 1980, p. 49.

20. *Annual,* SBC, 1982, p. 58.

21. "Conversations in Southern Baptist Life, Part I: Roots," *Missions USA,* 54:44, January-February 1983.

22. *Annual,* SBC, 1984, p. 60; *SBC Bulletin,* 13 June 1985, p. 5.

23. *Annual,* District of Columbia Baptist Convention, 1962, p. 53.

24. *Annual,* Baptist General Convention of Texas, 1962, p. 29.

25. *Annual,* Baptist General Association of Virginia, 1962, p. 63.

26. See, for example, ibid., 1963, pp. 62-62; 1964, p. 68; 1970, p. 107; 1971, p. 89; 1980, p. 45; 1981, pp. 47-48; 1982, pp. 50-51.

27. See, for example, *Annual,* Baptist General Convention of Texas, 1971, p. 22; 1980, pp. 71-72; 1982, p. 71; and *Annual,* Louisiana Baptist Convention, 1980, p. 175; 1981, p. 180; 1982, p. 186.

28. *Annual,* Baptist State Convention of North Carolina, 1982, pp. 108-09.

29. *Annual,* Kansas-Nebraska Convention of Southern Baptists, 1982, p. 12.

30. *Annual,* Alabama Baptist Convention, 1982, p. 80.

31. *Annual,* Kentucky Baptist Convention, 1982, p. 168.

32. *Annual,* Louisiana Baptist Convention, 1982, p. 186.

33. *Annual,* Missouri Baptist Convention, 1982, p. 78.

34. *Annual,* Tennessee Baptist Convention, 1982, p. 162.

35. *Annual,* Baptist General Convention of Texas, 1982, p. 71.

36. *Annual,* Baptist General Association of Virginia, 1982, p. 50.

37. Stan Hastey and Larry Chesser, "BJCPA Issues Warnings on School Prayer, Convention," *Baptist Press,* 4 March 1982, p. 1.

38. Stan Hastey, "Dunn Challenges Reagan on School Prayer Amendment," *Baptist Press,* 6 May 1982, p. 4.

39. Stan Hastey and Larry Chesser, "School Prayer Supporters Pledge No New Orleans Fight," *Baptist Press,* 10 May 1982, p. 1.

40. Presnall H. Wood, "Keep State Out of Prayer Writing Business," *Baptist Standard,* 19 May 1982, p. 8.

41. J. B. Fowler, "Religion and Prayer in the School Classroom," *Baptist New Mexican,* 5 June 1982, p. 2.

42. Stan Hastey, "McAteer Had White House Backing to Seek SBC Act," *Baptist Press,* 1 July 1982, p. 3.

43. "Allen Charges Coercion in School Prayer Amendment," *Baptist Press,* 28 July 1982, p. 2.

44. "Noted Baptist Leader Calls Prayer Amendment 'A False Bill of Goods,'" *The Christian Index,* 26 August 1982, p. 2.

45. Bob Terry, "A Look at the School Prayer Amendment," *Word and Way,* 26 August 1982, p. 2; Edgar R. Cooper, "Government Control of Religion? Reagan's Prayer Amendment Would Give Us Just That," *Florida Baptist Witness,* 9 December 1982, pp. 4-5.

46. Gene Puckett, "Discussing the Issues," *Biblical Recorder,* 8 January 1983, p. 2.

47. Stan Hastey, "Reagan Proposes Revised School Prayer Amendment," *Baptist Press,* 13 July 1983, p. 10.

48. C. R. Daley, "Guest Editorial: A Stand for Free Exercise," *Biblical Recorder,* 18 February 1984, p. 2.

49. See, e.g., "Religion Sponsored by the State," 4:141-49, November 1962; "Religion and Public Education in Historical Perspective," 14:397-414, Autumn 1972; and "Legislating Prayer in the Public Schools," 23:205-13, Spring 1981.

50. "Religion Sponsored by the State," p. 141.

51. "Religion and Public Education in Historical Perspective," p. 405.

52. "Legislating Prayer in the Public Schools," p. 211.

53. Ibid., p. 213.

54. "Summary of Carlson's Testimony on Dirksen Prayer Amendment," *Report from the Capital,* 21:6, August 1966.

55. James M. Sapp, "The School Prayer Issue," *Report from the Capital,* 26:2, September 1971.

56. Ibid.

57. W. Barry Garrett, "Court Decisions Since 1963," *Report from the Capital,* 26:2, October 1971.

58. "BJCPA's Dunn Challenges Reagan on Public School Prayer Amendment," *Report from the Capital,* 37:8, June 1982.

59. James M. Dunn, "Reflections," *Report from the Capital,* 37:15, July-August 1982.

60. John W. Baker, "Views of the Wall," *Report from the Capital,* 37:6, July-August 1982.

61. Stan Hastey, "Who Writes the Prayer? Amendment Avoids Saying," *Report from the Capital,* 38:16, September 1983.

CHAPTER 5

1. Wayne E. Oates, "Pastoral Counseling and the Experience of Prayer," *An Introduction to Pastoral Counseling,* Wayne E. Oates, ed. (Nashville: Broadman Press, 1959), p. 217.

Index